Wire Wrapping Book for Beginners

An Instruction Guide to Craft 15 Intricate Wire Wrapped and Bead Making Jewelry Designs With Tools and Techniques Included

By

Hattie Dolton

Copyright © 2021 – Hattie Dolton

All rights reserved

No part of this publication may be reproduced, distributed, or transmitted in any form or by any means, including photocopying, recording, or other electronic or mechanical methods, without the prior written permission of the publisher, except in the case of brief quotations embodied in reviews and certain other non-commercial uses permitted by copyright law.

Disclaimer

This publication is designed to provide competent and reliable information regarding the subject matter covered. However, the views expressed in this publication are those of the author alone, and should not be taken as expert instruction or professional advice. The reader is responsible for his or her own actions.

The author hereby disclaims any responsibility or liability whatsoever that is incurred from the use or application of the contents of this publication by the purchaser or reader. The purchaser or reader is hereby responsible for his or her own actions.

Table of Contents

Introduction 7

Chapter 1 9

Wire Wrapping Fundamentals 9

    What is Wire Wrapping Jewelry? 9

    How Does It Work? 10

    History Of Wire Wrapping Jewelry 12

    What Objects Can You Wrap? 14

Chapter 2 18

Wire Wrapping Tips For Jewelry Making 18

Chapter 3 25

Techniques In Wire Wrapped Jewelry 25

    Twisting Wire 25

    Basic Anchor Loop 26

    Wrapping Wire 27

    Coils 28

    Weaving 32

    Loop Joins 34

    Wire Beads 35

    Hook and Eye Clasp 36

    Hardening 38

Chapter 4 40

Getting Started With Wire Wrapped Jewelry 40

    Tools and Materials 40

        Jewelry Wire 40
        Gemstone Beads 46
        Gemstones 55
        Flush Cutters 57
        Pliers 57
        Ruler 60
        Permanent Marker 61
        Files 62
        Chasing Hammer 62
        Vise 63
        Steel Bench Block 64
        Mandrels 64
        Metal Hole Punch 65
        Crimp Tool 66
        Jigs 66

Setting Up Your Wire Wrapped Jewelry Studio 67

Wire Wrapping Jewelry Safety Precautions 73

Chapter 5 78

Wire Wrapped Jewelry Projects 78

    Wire Wrapped Cabochon Pendant 78

    Wire Wrapped Bead Rings 89

    Wire Wrapped Bead Bracelet 93

    Wire Wrapped Bead Earrings 96

    Crystal Wrapped Cuff Bracelet 104

    Beaded Wire Heart Necklace 108

    Crescent Moon Wire Wrapped Necklace 113

    Folded Wired Ring 119

    Zen Wired Spiral Pendant 127

    Birch Leaf Wired Earrings 131

    Wire Bangle Beaded Bracelets 139

    Swirled Wire Ear Cuff 144

    Wire Wrapped Headband 148

Spiral Wire Bookmark 151

Wire Wrapped Bead Chain 155

Chapter 6 160

Wire Wrapped Jewelry Mistakes To Avoid 160

Chapter 7 169

Wire Wrapped Jewelry FAQs 169

Conclusion 175

Introduction

Wire wrapping jewelry is becoming a popular craft these days because of its simplicity and accessibility. Of course, it is very affordable and quite easy to make, so the increase in the demand for wire wrapping jewelry is not a surprise at all. Learning to make wire wrapping jewelry saves you the extra cost of buying pieces of jewelry all the time. You can make amazing jewelry to gift someone you deeply love and watch them rock it. In the jewelry world, a standout trick is to stay unique. You can't be unique if you do what every other person is doing, even if it is a trend. Breathe your own style into the art; that is how magic is birthed.

There are several wire wrapping jewelry designs, both simple and complicated alike. However, before you start making these designs, you need to be educated on the techniques, tips, and tricks used in wrapping wire. Also, you need to get accustomed to projects that illustrate these basic techniques before you start wrapping really complex designs or creating your own designs. Some of these basic designs are discussed in this book, with well-explained steps on creating them. With every step made easy, you are sure to get started in your wire wrapping practice soon enough. All the tools you need to start are discussed, putting you one step closer to being an awesome jewelry crafter.

Making wire wrapping jewelry can be so exciting for many reasons. You can't imagine the excitement that would come when people actually compliment something you made with your own hands; trust me, the feeling is awesome. Although you might feel caught up as a beginner, however, you've just got yourself the right book to navigate you through the murky waters of wire wrapping. On the pages of this book, you will be exposed to how you can move from a novice to an expert in the art of wire wrapping jewelry.

So, let's get right into it!

Chapter 1

Wire Wrapping Fundamentals

What is Wire Wrapping Jewelry?

Just like the term indicates or suggests, wire wrapping is simply wrapping wire around wire or on any other object like beads and fine stones to create jewelry. Quite complex, right? However, wrapping wire on a wire is usually done to create a loop to bring in other components and join them together to make jewelry. These loops can be a simple wire loop or a wrapped pendant. Wire wrapping can also be done to adjust beads to a certain form and give them a unique shape. Wire can also be wrapped on other non-bead items to change its look and make it into a new form just like wrapping a series of rhinestone cups to curve into a bangle.

When the wire has been manipulated through curving, bending, and wrapping, this wire is now the foundation for you to build any piece of design of your choice. Wire wrapping gives you a great chance to be creative because of its easily manipulative feature that allows you to create unique shapes, angles, and designs just the way you imagined them to be.

How Does It Work?

There are different strengths and textures of wires used in wire wrapping. However, all these wires are flexible and bendable into varieties of shapes or forms or patterns. The round-nose pliers are commonly used to make cuts at certain bends or reducing the wire's length to a more suitable one, depending on the project type you are working on. Cutters like the round-nose pliers are also useful for removing loose ends.

There is no one style or medium of wire wrapping. At different points, artisans and jewelry makers have come up with unique techniques for wire wrapping. These techniques include very organized and orderly patterns for wrapping fine stones, beads, or gem stones. These patterns include arranging different pieces of wire and wrapping them on each other with a small gauge until they form a single wide band. Finally, the gemstone is used to loop around the wide band. After the loop has been made, the round-nose pliers are slightly used to pull out a single wire on either side of the loop. This wire is used to form firm support in the stone to keep it from falling out through the back or front.

Most artists use this method; however, modern wire wrappers seem to be carving out a technique for themselves: a freestyle approach and a simple pattern. It allows for deep imaginations and a sharp sense of aesthetic balance to guide the movement of their hands as the wrapping takes place. This technique insists on the need for cultivating intuition, structural integrity, and firmness. The stone must be firmly kept in position to prevent it from falling. One sure way of preventing the stone from falling out is by closing all the possible loopholes.

As wonderful as this wrapping method appears, especially because of its flexibility, all the other ways of wrapping are unique in their own way. Hence, no one can say this is the perfect way to wrap wire. Every technique is as good as the other if you know how to use it. Funnily, this is what makes wire wrapping a popular craft; you can be flexible about the methods of carrying out the craft. Most importantly, having the right patience, imagination, and physical stability to engage in major designs. Even after adopting a technique, every artist owns it and makes it theirs by applying that technique in their own style.

The way and manner artist A carries out technique A is super different from how artist B carries out technique A. it is rare to come by two artists who have used the same technique and style. Wire wrapping gives a chance for ingenuity and uniqueness. This is what makes an outstanding craft.

One less appreciated fact about wire wrapping is that it is very relaxing and soothing. You are putting your mind and body to work in a relaxed condition and without making so many demands from your body. However, you need to be mentally focused with a meditative mindset to monitor the unfolding of your wrapping/wiring. You practically can't perform well when your mind is destabilized and unsettled.

Unlike other crafts that require huge capital investment to start and get established. Wire wrapping involves just basic tools and materials that almost everyone can afford. Wire wrapping is one of the simplest, easiest, and most interesting ways of making jewelry. You are most definitely out to enjoy the process and become a skilled jewelry maker.

History Of Wire Wrapping Jewelry
Wire wrapping has been going on for several years. It is a top feature of human civilization in Ancient Egypt,

over 4,300 years ago. Around that time, jewelry making was done with gold, silver and copper because they could be easily flexed and bent into any form. Also, wire came from hitting and folding these materials into slim sheets of metals, cut them into small strips, and tube them by rolling them slowly to form a wire.

This was all before the intense growth and development of technology. Ancient artisans could still find a way to create beautiful work from scratch, all with their hands. Hence, as time began to pass and advancements were introduced, more artisans began to initiate unique techniques for wrapping wire.

Still, around the millennia, there was slow progress in the practice of wire wrapping until a certain artist, Alexander Calder and Ruth Asawa, two award-winning and amazing jewelry makers began using wires to make interesting pieces of jewelry. Hence, they reintroduced the uniqueness of the craft and the amazing versatility of the wire. The flexibility in use was also a unique factor for consideration.

They revealed that wires can be used to trace the lines in sculptures and reproduce something similar or exact in appearance. Also, online selling platforms have a customized function for people who know how to make jewelry through wire wrapping. Hence, you are not just making some fancy stuff to be admired; you can make some good bucks out of your sweat and creativity by registering on one of those platforms like Folksy. This is most amazing for a craft that doesn't require much capital to start, long hours of commitment, complicated tools, and techniques in making it.

The simplicity and versatility of this craft are a top factor that has made it popular and appreciated. Today, many people are picking an interest in learning how they can make aesthetic objects through wire wrapping.

What Objects Can You Wrap?

Wrapping objects to produce jewelry requires some level of skill and mastery of certain techniques. However, you need to know that you can wrap virtually anything with a shape and a form with wire. You only need to apply care, severity, and perseverance in making it aesthetic and acceptable. Since everything with shape or form can be wrapped, you stand to experience difficulty when using certain objects to make them aesthetic. Some shapes are tough to wrap in wire but not impossible. With the right training, knowledge and experience, anyone can wrap anything, no matter how difficult.

However, flat objects appear to be easier to wrap than most rounding objects, especially spherical objects. Objects with openings or holes are easier to wrap than plain objects with smooth surfaces without any openings. This is because the opportunity to pass the wire through the hole makes it less stressful to make certain designs and to give the wire a natural bend. Also, it helps you to achieve stabilization for your piece. This is why many persons prefer wrapping large beads to small stones. Another preference in wrapping is strength. It is best to wrap objects that are strong than those that are not. When wrapping weak or breakable objects, you need to be extra careful in the process of wrapping and avoid using wires with very tough textures.

Here is a brief list of objects that can be easily wrapped with wire

- Beads: the most common beads are larger glass and resin beads. They are commonly used for making pendants and other aesthetic materials for jewelry.
- Simple stones: these are fine smooth, hard and simple stones with a small hole of one inch at the center. In some cases, the stone might have a

diameter of two inches. These stones are usually flatter than the normal round stones; hence wrapping them is just as easy as it can be.
- Sea glass: this is a flat material used in making aesthetic crafts and designs. It is not too brittle; hence, a wire can easily go over it. Given its flat features also, it is a good place to start wrapping.
- Keys: this is the most popularly used objects by beginners. They are quite easy to wrap because of their flatness, simplicity and center holes.

Other complicated objects for wire wrapping include;

- Gemstones: these are round, strong and flake-able stones. It doesn't have holes in its centers. They are naturally appealing to the eyes and amazing to behold.
- Chops of driftwood: this wood is quite fragile and could threaten to break if you don't handle it carefully.
- Shells: this is in a challenging class of its own. Given its shape, it is very difficult to wrap wire about it successfully. However, upon completion, it is one of the most beautiful pieces of jewelry

you can make through wire wrapping. Shells are just complicated and beautiful.

Finally, as earlier mentioned, you can wrap any object of any shape. Every object is a potential tool to create wrap-able art; you just need to be skilled in using the techniques and have the right knowledge.

Chapter 2

Wire Wrapping Tips For Jewelry Making

1. File the ends of your wire: when you are wrapping wire for jewelry, you want to make sure the wire is smooth or reduce the aesthetics of the jewelry. To have a smooth, shiny jewelry piece at the end of your work, ensure to file the end of your wire after you make any cut. Also, for ear jewelry, it is most essential that you file the ends of your wire or risk getting your ears injured from the rough mouthpiece of the wire.

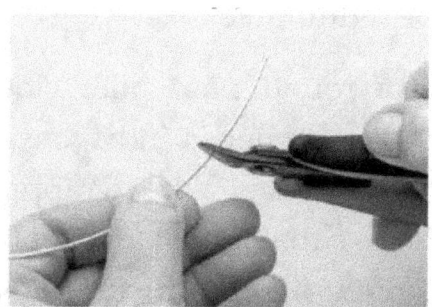

Wires can be dangerous when it is rough, if it comes in contact with a human's body, it can cause scratches and injury to the person wearing it. You won't want your customers to get injured by your jewelry. To file the ends of your wire, make use of a cup bur or a wire file.

2. Make use of a flush cutter: flush cutters are used to achieve flush cuts, and as obvious as that might sound, this could be a big deal for your wire wrapping project. After you have wrapped the jewelry object with your wire and are ready to make a cut, use a flush cutter to cut the end. You will have one flush, straight cut side and a pointed cut side when you do this. The visible wire at the end of your work should be the flush wire with a straight ending. It gives your work a form of straightness and smoothness that's simply admirable.

3. Keep a round nose plier close: the value of a round nose plier is indispensable when you are working on any wire wrapping project. Hence, make sure that the plier is kept close as you work. You might find it difficult to make tight wraps or close ring seams that look uniform. A round nose plier is a great tool that can be used in addressing this difficulty. Make a visible mark on a particular point on the plier using a scriber or marker. Use

your pliers in forming loops and the mark on the plier would act as a borderline for making consistent loops all the time. Unlike when you were using just your hands, you don't need to guess; you can be sure of making accurate and tight loops.

4. Imperceptible jump ring seams: when making jump rings, make sure it is closed tightly and neatly. There should be no space between two jump rings. To check the tightness of your jump rings, run your hands over them. If it is tight, you would not feel spaces between the rings.

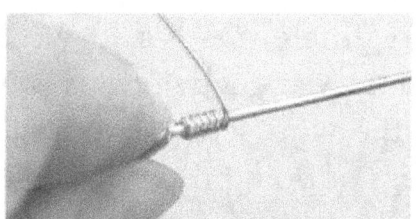

5. Keep wraps tight: wrapped loops and coils are the first techniques you should practice in wire jewelry making. In your practice, endeavor to make the wraps tight and closed up against each other. Also, if you are making a pair of jewelry, you should have the same number of wraps in

each pair. For instance, the double pair of earrings should have the same number of wraps. Upon your last wrap, use a plier to squeeze and tighten it firmly so it doesn't loosen or stick out. Also, you can hide the wrapped loop by snipping it to the side of the coil.

6. Work harden your wire after wrapping: hardening is what gives your wire the stability to last for several years and stay ready to wear. By work hardening your wire, you are applying force on the wire to make it hard and strong enough to hold its shape.

There are different ways to work harden your wire to make a good jewelry design. You can hammer the wire softly with a strong mallet. In the process of doing this, you are beating out air from the wire, so strength and texture can build up the inner frame of the wire.

Another method involves using a pair of pliers to make twists with the wire and straightening it out several times. This can be done after you have completed your design; it is best done before wrapping the wire or making the design.

7. Make close loops when wrapping a gemstone: gemstones are uniquely different from other stones and could be quite a concern when wrapping. However, all concerns could be settled by making close loops to keep the stones in place. Your close loops don't have to be conventional and plain. You can make creative loops that are still tight and functional. In the later chapters, we would look at how to make unique loops.

8. Nonetheless, you would need to constantly try out different ways of keeping a gemstone firmly locked in a wrap. For every gemstone, the challenge could be different. If you will want to keep your gemstone jewelry in good shape, learn close loops designs.

9. Master the different available tensile strengths of wires and validate before you make a purchase: there are different wire strengths. Some are very malleable, half-hard and very rigid. You need to identify the type of wire and the required tensile strength for the project you are working on before purchasing the wrong wire. Also, note that wire strength is also affected by the gauge of the wire.

A soft wire with a large wire gauge will still be stiff. So, look out for tensile strength and wire gauge.

10. Be careful when weaving on an angled frame: when weaving, start from the end at the narrowest point of the frame and continue weaving from there until you get to the widest end of the frame. If you weave the other way round, the wire could loosen at some point and slip down the frame.

11. Select a strong wire gauge when wrapping stones; Wrapping stones could be unusually technical. However, it could be made a lot easier if you follow certain principles like selecting a strong wire gauge. Stones are hard and heavy; they need something strong and hardened to hold them in place. You need a wire that will be strong enough to hold it firm and flexible enough to loop around the stone creatively and properly. The best gauge size for wrapping stones is 20. This wire is strong and malleable at the same time. It doesn't break so easily. An example of a 20-gauge wire is the copper wire. It is very much

affordable and makes a very good wire for wrapping stones.

12. Use the right tools and supplies when replicating a design: when replicating designs from a tutorial, endeavor to use the right tools and supplies mentioned in the tutorial. If you didn't note it down, you might have to revisit the tutorial to note the tools and supplies used because as a beginner there are certain things you can't figure out on your own, like the type of wire to use in a certain project. Replicating a design with the wrong supplies could put you in s frustrating dilemma and cause you to hurt your fingers. The best solution is to watch/ re-watch the tutorial while you practice the design. When the tutorial happens to be in a book like this, endeavor to read and re-read the book while practicing the design, allow yourself to be guided by the tutor. This way you are sure of a better result.

Chapter 3

Techniques In Wire Wrapped Jewelry

Wires are flexible and malleable materials that can be made into various shapes. There are different techniques for flexing wires. They are explained explicitly below;

Twisting Wire

Unlike other malleable objects that become weak when twisted together, the wire becomes stronger when twisted. It also increases in strength and texture. Soft wires are always easier to twist like copper, unlike harder wires which require careful effort and caution when twisting. An example of harder wires is the galvanized wire.

When twisting wires, take a firm hold on them; letting go can cause the wire to spin out of control and loosen your loop.

To exercise control over your wire while you twist, make use of a hand drill. This will enable you to have firm control over the wire. When you are just beginning your twist, ensure your wire is three times as long as your required length, this is because the more you twist, the more wire you need. Fold the wire well into two and hang it on a door handle. Ensure that the surface of your wire is protected from scratches. Secure the wire ends with a cup hook. Now grip the wire taut and use a drill to move the door handle so that you are slowly twisting the wire.

If you don't have a drill, you would have to get one or modify one from a wooden coat hanger with a revolving wire hook. Cut out a wire three times the length of desired final length. Then repeat the process of folding the wire in twos so that the two ends are touching each other. Loop the wire on the door handle. Now wrap the ends thrice around the hanger. When the wire is taut, start to rotate the coat hanger. To make an even twist, place a firm grip on the wire horizontally. Now, twist the wire to the desired degree. Make sure you are not over twisting or you might get to lose your wire in the twist by a snap. Separate your wire from the drill or door handle and cut the ends of the wire.

Basic Anchor Loop

This is one of the foundational loops you are expected to learn as a beginner. To make this loop, grab the end of the wire using a round-nose plier. Place the wire at four inches from the nose of the plier while you hold the plier firmly. With your firm hold on the plier's handles, form a tight loop at the wire's end by pulling the wire around or turning the plier slightly. Move the loop to the tip of the plier and squeeze it to flatten out the end.

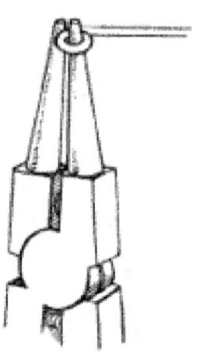

Wrapping Wire

When wrapping two wires together, the base wire should be stronger than the wrapping wire. If you want to use two wires of the same texture, you have to select a soft wire like copper. Because some wires are so strong that using them to wrap would be impossible or difficult, you must have decided the length you want your final product to be, but when cutting the base or core wire, ensure to cut an extra two inches to all your already decided length. This will be used in forming a winding loop. If the length is too much to manage, ensure to coil the ends before you start wrapping.

To make this loop, you only need to make an anchor loop like explained above, using a round nose plier. Afterward, attach your wrapping wire.

Now that you have made your loop, place a thin object like a pencil inside the loop and rotate the wire with one hand. This is called winding. While you are doing this, you want to ensure your wire is well wrapped. Scrunch and tighten the wire coils with one hand while you rotate the loop.

Coils

A commonly used decorative shape that adds style to your designs while eliminating sharp end hazards

- Coiling closed coils: this is one type of decorative coil that is formed to achieve uniqueness and hide the sharp hazardous end of the wire. This coil is made by creating a small loop at the tail end of the wire using a round-nosed plier. Use a channel-type plier to hold the loop firmly and begin to move the wire to bend around itself. To make a tight coil, adjust the position of the plier as you work and ensure that you move the wire with sufficient pressure. However, be careful not to mar the wire by bending it so hard or exerting so much pressure.

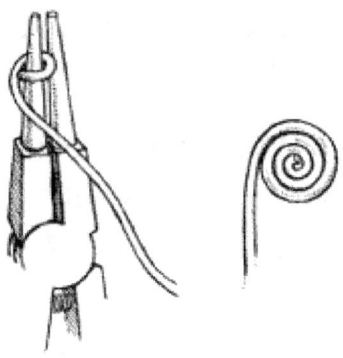

- Open coils: the difference between this coil and the former one is that this one allows for thin space after every two coils. Form a loop at the end of the wire using a round nose plier as you did above. Ensure the plier is holding the loop firmly. Then, use your thumb to push the wire, so it forms a curve. Make the necessary adjustment to have the exact space you need between the rings of the coil. Use a channel plier to flatten the arrangement of the coils when you are done.

- Flattened extended coils: this is a unique coil type used to make structural designs for containers and other fancy metals. It is a very fast and easy way to create a decorative trim.

To create this unique coil above, wrap the wire around the broomstick several times until you have a coil of your desired length. Wrap the wire until the coil is as long as you desire. Then gently and slowly splay out the loops by stretching from the two ends of the wire. Flatten the loop by using your fingers and thumb to hold the loops one by one. Another spaying option is to use a nylon jaw plier to squeeze a small group of coils. Continue this process until the coils are well flattened. This will give your loop an oval shape in place of a round shape.

Tip: You can also make a dimensional coil by making a wrap around a dowel to make a coil. Remove the wire when you are done wrapping and use a jaw plier to tuck in the sharp ends of the wire to make the coil malleable or flexible to suit any shape.

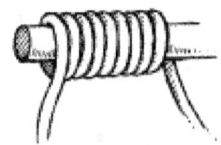

Tip: Place the blunt edge of a butter knife between the coils and rotate this coil using the blade of the knife. This will evenly separate wire coils slightly

- Scrollwork or ribbon coils:

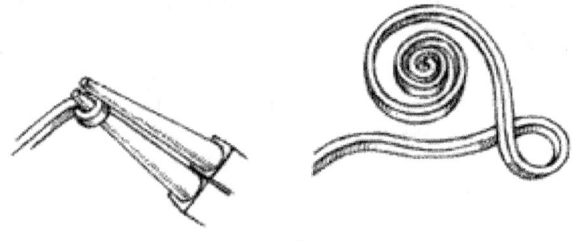

Get a pretty hard flat surface, place your wire on it, and flatten it into a ribbon shape by hammering it until it's flat. Use the plier to shape the wire around the plier's jaw. Adjust the pliers slightly, so it forms a coil as you move. To incorporate the coil as a part of other wire pieces, use nylon jaw pliers.

Weaving

This is a cloth-making technique commonly used in making baskets and textile designs. Weaving requires a soft, pliable, and multicolored wire like the fine enameled copper wire. This wire is the most suitable for wire weaving. There are different ways to weave.

The easiest way is to wind wire under struts and spokes. The winding should move over and under the struts. To create struts, make cuts of equal lengths of wire and fold them in a loose manner halfway or at certain points of intersection. Join these wires together, and hold them at the center in one hand. After that, attach a long wire to it and start weaving around the wire. Make the weaving in an over/under fashion round the circle as you go. Move the wire three times around the spoke and splice the wire's tail to add to the spoke. Add a new wire to the spoke, close to the one that is already weaving, and adjust it into a pattern. As you weave, spread the spokes in an organized circle as you go.

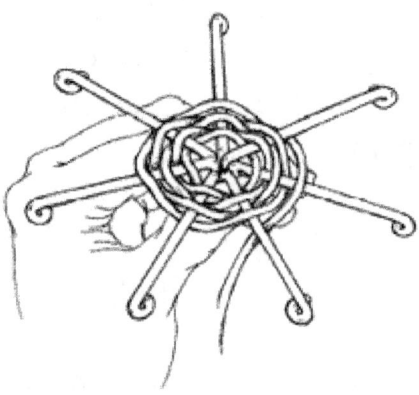

For a more aesthetic and smoother finish, make an even number of weaves of spokes or struts. Get a long wire and begin to weave around the struts making loops on the wire struts by passing the wire over consistently. Do this till the wire is exhausted to have a smooth surface.

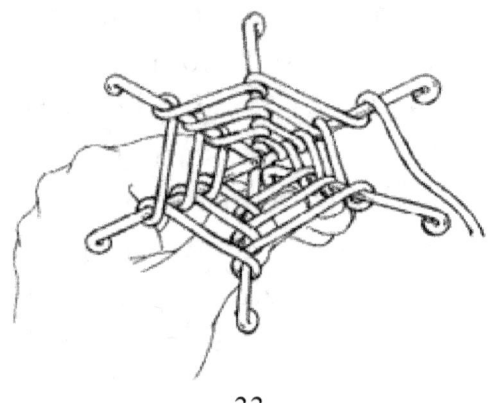

This weave is the reverse of the previous technique. You make the weave under the struts by passing the wire under the struts and making the loops. This will create a pattern of ridges in the weave.

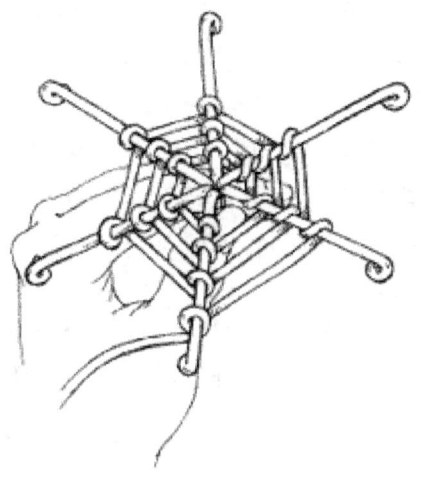

Loop Joins

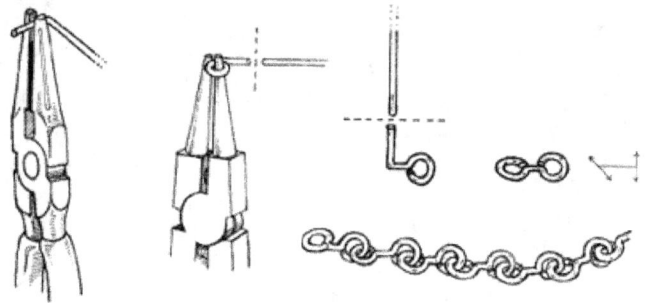

This is a technique for joining two pieces of wire together. This technique is most especially used in making a chain, or links of a chain. To achieve this, use a round nose plier to create figure-eight loops like in the picture. To make a figure-eight loop, bend the tips of a wire at a 90-degree angle using a flat nose plier. Now, make the loop from the bent tip using a round nose plier. Then use a flat nose plier to bend the wire at a 90-degree angle then cut the wire at that length. Repeat this procedure until you create enough figure-eight loops. Then join the loops together through the flat nose pliers by creating small openings in the loop to link them together. Thereafter the joining, be careful to close the loops again with the flat nose plier. Do not apply too much pressure so as not to unwind the loops.

Wire Beads

In this technique, individual wires are twisted to form the round shape of a ball of yarn. To make this ball, you need to get 24 inches of wire with a gauge size of 18. Make a loop at one end of the wire. Then bend the wire at two inches below the loop; this wire will act as the center post for wrapping the whole body. Hold the wire with a plier and start wrapping using your hands to make the wire round about the center post. Wrap the wire like you would wrap a string ball. If you want it tight, wrap it tightly. Don't be stiff with the position of the plier; keep moving it round the ball as you wrap. The pliers are mostly useful for also adjusting the wraps and helping to ensure it is as tight or as loose as you desire. When you must have achieved the ball size you desire, move the end of the wire inside the ball and string it in there. Ensure that it comes out at the opposite end of the ball. Afterward, create a loop from that end of the wire. So you have two loops opposite each other.

Hook and Eye Clasp

Get a six inches wire and bend it tightly in the middle against itself using the flat nose pliers. Use the round nose pliers to form a bend at the base of the folded wire at two inches from the wire. Use the flat nose pliers to separate the two wires so that they are opposite each other, just like no.3 in the picture illustrates. Then use one of the two wires to wrap the two wires together by creating a tight coil around them. When wrapping, hold the wire with a flat nose plier to prevent it from moving around. Now trim any excess wire. Then create a loop with the small wire. Then attach the rings of the coil using this loop. For you to ensure that a ring goes with the hook, measure 2 inches of wire and wrap it around the base of the round pliers. Use the plier to adjust the circle until you have a coil of about ¼ diameter. Then create a split ring with an overlapping end. Remove the excesses and tighten the ring with a flat nose plier.

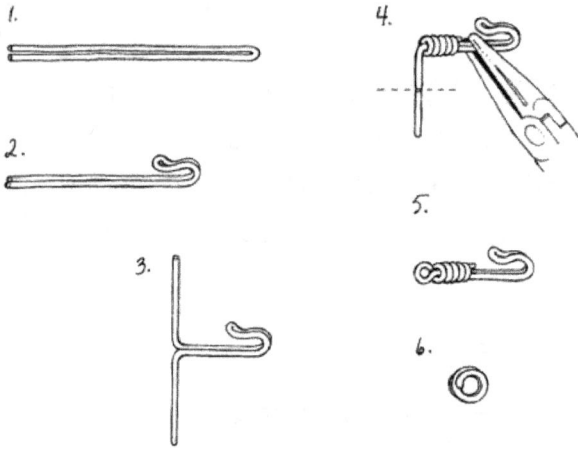

Tip: To prevent a lot of tweaking when making the split ring, rotate at least three times, and trim it down so that the end overlaps well.

Hardening

This is the process of increasing the texture of the wire by stiffening it. This way, the wire is made firmer than ever. One uncommon way of hardening wire is using the nylon jaw plier to flatten the metal by hitting it repeatedly without changing the diameters. There are two types of nylon jaw pliers; regular and thin nose pliers. Just like the name indicates, the thin nose plier is used for hardening tight places. Moving the wire in a particular position over time will stiffen the wire and harden it, locking up the shape of the design. Also, a mallet or chasing hammer can be used in hammering the wire to make it harder. Hammering is also done to flatten the wire and the design and to texturize the wire.

A Short message from the Author:

Hey, I hope you are enjoying the book? I would love to hear your thoughts!

Many readers do not know how hard reviews are to come by and how much they help an author.

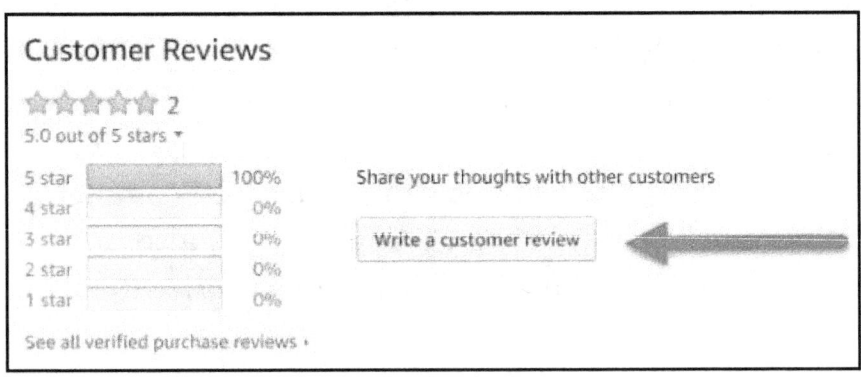

I would be incredibly grateful if you could take just 60 seconds to write a short review on Amazon, even if it is a few sentences!

\>> Click here to leave a quick review

Thanks for the time taken to share your thoughts!

Chapter 4

Getting Started With Wire Wrapped Jewelry

Tools and Materials

You must have gotten familiar with certain tools that have been mentioned in previous chapters, especially the pliers. However, you need more than a plier, your hands, and a wire to make wire-wrapped jewelry. Depending on the nature of your design or project, there is a whole lot of work that needs to go into pruning the wire to achieve your desired result. Same for the type of tools used in wire wrapping. You need specialized tools for special projects. Below is a long list of tools you need in making wire-wrapped jewelry.

Jewelry Wire

Not every type of wire can be used for jewelry because of its texture and gauges size. This goes a long way to affect their function and usability. There lies the dilemma; how do I know which wire is good enough for my jewelry type? Most artists or crafters still struggle to identify which of the wires work best for their selected project. However, we have gathered a list of factors worth considering before selecting a jewelry wire to reduce the pressure and make it less daunting.

- Wire shapes: there are different shapes of wires. This includes; half-round, round, square, and twisted. The twisted wire is incredible when used to create a spiraling effect. The square and half-round wires are best for wrapping materials like beads and stones; this is because they have a flat side that keeps the wire-wrapped object from falling off. The round wires are most versatile and can serve any wrapping purpose.

- Wire materials: wire materials refer to the components and features of the wire that makes them capable of fitting certain tasks. These materials refer to not just components but lifespan, price, color and durability. Wire materials are usually characterized as steel, brass, silver, nickel, copper, and gold. Gold and silver are mostly expensive and rarely used except for special jewelry designs. All these wires come in different colors. The most common colors are black, blue, red, green, purple. Copper can be found in all these colors. Hence, it is the frequently used wire; however, it appears plain and too simple. In most cases, it could be combined with a more attractive wire like gold or silver. Brass is tricky to use in designing because it is quite springy. If its use is well mastered, it could give you a really unique design.

- Wire strength: there are three categories of wire strength; full hard, half-hard, and dead soft.

    a. Full hard: this is the toughest wire. It is also very thick and robust because of the pressure to pass through the draw plate several times. Also, it is very firm and hardly ever loses shape.

    b. Half-hard: this wire has also been pulled through the draw plate severally, which made it tough. The difference between this wire and the full hard wire is that the full hard wire was pulled through the draw plate a few more times than the half-hard wire. This wire is commonly used because it is malleable and firm.

- c. Dead soft: this is the softest wire type and it can be easily bent with the bare hands by just a little exertion of pressure. It is best prescribed for beginners in the craft of wire wrapping, as it enables them to achieve more by exerting little pressure. However, you can't count on its firmness; the jewelry might start to lose shape after a while.

- Wire gauge: this is the measure of wire thickness. A very thick wire is usually hard to bend and stays very firm after being folded or wrapped. What then is the best wire gauge that can be used in wrapping stones? There are various levels of wire gauge in the market. This makes it difficult to settle on which wire gauge is appropriate for your project. However, we have included a couple of familiar wire gauges and how they can be efficiently used in wrapping stones for different designs and projects;

  - a. 16-18 Gauge: this is a commonly used gauge for jewelry that requires a framework, especially bracelets and pendants. They help to keep your framework sturdy and structurally firm. However, they are also excellent for sculpting because they are tough to bend and maintain their shape over time.

b. 20-22 Gauge: this wire is commonly used in establishing embellishments and setting up stable frameworks.

c. 20-24 Gauge: this is much thinner and pliable. It is easily bendable and doesn't tend to maintain shape for so long. Hence, it is best used for fine detailing and not wrapping frameworks.

Having considered these features or necessary factors to look out for when selecting a wrapping wire, we need to also understand the available wrapping wires. This will make the selection an easier choice. There are only two wires discussed in this section, but there is much more than these if you search the market. However, you can trust these wires for functionality sake;

a. Benecreat Various Metal Wire: this wire comes in four distinct colors; gold, silver, copper, antique bronze. It comes in rolls and packages. A roll contains 11 yards of 20-gauge wire and a package contains four rolls of each of the four colors listed above. Coated with a tarnish-resistant coating, this wire is known to maintain its color and shine for a very long time. It stays forever fashionable and stays durable for several years. Also, it is very pliable and flexible, making it easy to use when working on long projects or starting off as a beginner. However, you can't trust that it won't lose its shape after a very long time because of its pliability.

b. Bare Copper Wire For Hobby Craft: this wire is just as homely and warm as its name sounds. It is a great option for beginners to help them master the act of wire wrapping. This wire is flexible and very soft. As pliable as it is, you can use them to wrap just about anything without having to worry about stressing the wire or causing it to break. You can also use a hammer or solder to solder it with another wire without breaking due to its firmness. This is 25 feet of 20-gauge wire with solid copper of up to 99.95%.

Beads: these are commonly used in making jewelry from wire wrapping because of their affordability and accessibility. Beads are pretty small shapes that come in a variety of shapes and sizes. These sizes range from very tiny pieces of small millimeters to chunky-sized beads. Beads are usually threaded on tiny ropes or strings to make basic jewelry pieces. You can make fashionable pieces of jewelry just by stringing beads together. There are different types of beads, categorized based on their material type, shape, grade, origin, surface pattern, production process and shape. In the next section, the most common beads are discussed, and their categories are well highlighted. Based on your project type, you can identify and select the beads most appropriate for you.

Gemstone Beads

This bead is also referred to as semi-precious beads. There are different types of gemstone beads ranging from natural gemstones to enhanced gemstones to manmade reconstructed materials. They come in various sizes and shapes. The shapes are endless; cabochons, faceted, smooth round, chips and nuggets of semi-precious stones with irregular shapes like amethyst, agate, and jade.

- Crystalove Crystals:

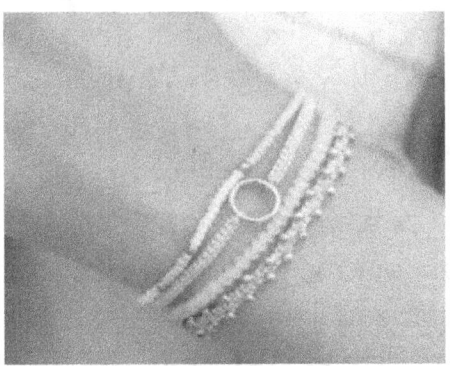

These beads are glass-like with a rainbow of colors. They also come in larger pack sizes with more beads than their rivals. This makes them a great choice for low-budget options. Also, they provide you a series of shapes and sizes. The common bead sizes are bicones, rondelles and rounds, amongst others. Bicone beads are usually diamond-shaped with aesthetics that make them appear like sparkles. You can only imagine how dazzling these beads can be when used to make jewelry. Rondelle beads are not as large as round beads. They are majorly used as spacers between beads. Although there are rondelle beads that come in crystals, there are also different sizes and shapes of rondelle beads.

- Matubo beads:

This bead is made with Preciosa Ornella glass with a special surface treatment technology. It also comes with unique coatings and high-purity holes. These holes are glossy and smooth on the surface, making them easier to string through. Matubo beads include gem duo beads, super duo, nib-bit beads and ginko beads.

- Firepolish beads:

These are really quality beads made from the Czech Republic. It is quite more expensive than other beads, but you can be sure to get great value for your money. The beads are machine-fired and faceted to give a unique and dazzling sparkle. These beads are usually produced under very high temperatures to make them appear like glass. There are several sizes of these beads.

- Natural pearls and shells:

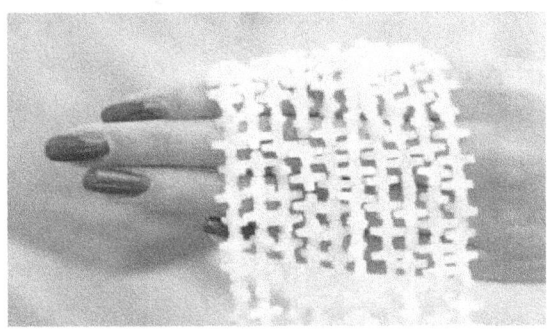

These pearls are usually gotten from saltwater or freshwater, and then they are made into beads. The pearls gotten from saltwater are always pinkish in color. In some other types of water, like fresh water, you can find pearls that are mauve in color, off-white and creamy. If heated under very high temperatures, these pearls could be made to look like glass, irrespective of their color, size, finishing, or shape.

- Crystal beads:

These beads are made from leaded glass that is why it has such a high shine. The highest crystal bead is the Swarovski bead that has a unique and appealing shine. It is usually used on wedding dresses and special jewelry. Swarovski has different elements under it, which include; rivoli, chatons, and flatbacks. A cheaper crystal is the Czech crystal bead. It is much more affordable and of lesser quality than Swarovski.

- Shamballa style beads:

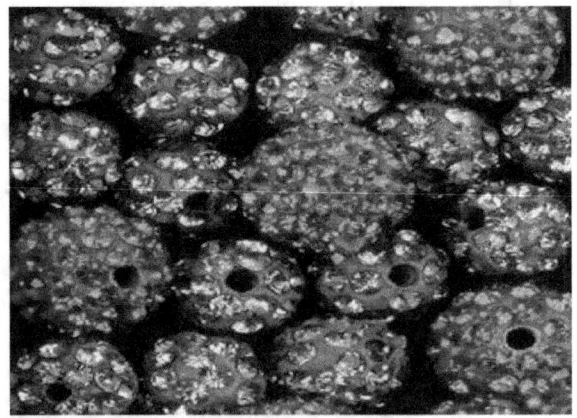

These beads are made with a clay base and Czech crystals to create an eye-catching bead. This bead is used in making a bracelet named the Shamballa.

- Milly beads:

These beads are made of glass with a shiny coating that makes them appear really lovely. It comes in rounds and rondelles shapes.

- Wooden beads:

These are uniquely pretty and uncommon designers beads. It gives your jewelry an earthy and crude touch. You can use them for making native necklaces or yoga-style necklaces.

- Bugle beads:

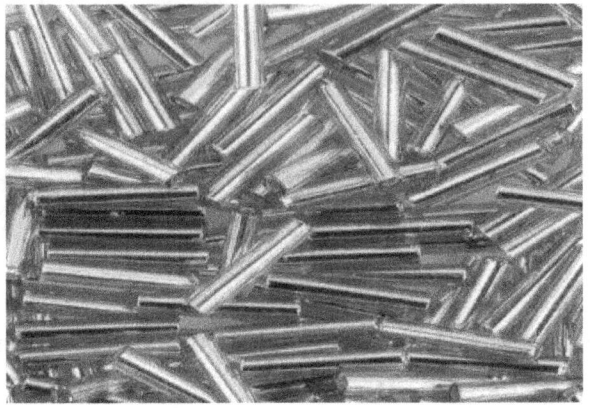

These beads are unlike other beads that have a circular or round shape. It comes in a tube shape. This tube is usually very long and then you can cut it to different lengths of your choice. They are very much useful in creating special bead jewelry and necklace.

Others are;

- Acrylic stones: these stones are popular beads that are most suitable for kid's craft because of their lightweight. Also, if you will be making designs with different patterns and long tails, you should consider using this as it allows you to use

so many beads without bearing the weight's bane or burden.
- CzechMates: these beads are made by heating Czech glass under very high temperatures. The temperature fashions it until it comes out in a fantastic geometric style and shapes like the petal-shaped dagger. These beads are very unique and highly flexible; they come with two to four holes in one bead. No design cannot be made with these beads; it allows for express innovation.
- Pony beads: these beads come in a seed-like shape. They are usually made of wood, plastic or glass. The glass beads are made by passing thick molten rods through an automatic pressing machine with the hand.
- Liquid beads: they come in silver or gold. These beads look like liquid when they are assembled together. It is very similar to the bugle beads and proves to be a great option for wrapping stranded wires.
- Crow beads: these beads also come in seed shape like the pony beads but in a much larger form. They could sometimes be mistaken for pony beads because they also income in glass form.

Well, the major difference is that they are larger than the pony beads.
- Cloisonné: these beads are fired enamel that has a mosaic glass effect. It is highly decorative and can be found in various shapes and sizes.
- Charlottes: these are a type of Czech seed beads that has one on its facets flat ground on the surface.
- Lampworked beads: they are handmade melted glass rods. These rods are melted with a flame torch. After it is melted, the molten glass is wrapped around a coated wire such that when it is removed, a hole is formed in that place. You can find this bead in so many colors.
- Les Perie Perse: made by a popular French jewelry artist, these beads are processed from high-quality Czech glass.

Gemstones

They are also called precious stones or fine gems. This is a mineral crystal piece cut and polished to make several adornments. Gemstones are rare and pretty hard to find, making them more expensive than the bead. Not only is it hard to find, but it also has a hard texture, and it is harder to wrap about, unlike the beads. Even when the stones are yet to be cut, it still looks good and is very much usable. Some of the common gemstones are diamonds, emeralds, sapphires, and rubies. These are used in making pieces of jewelry for a very special occasion.

Flush Cutters

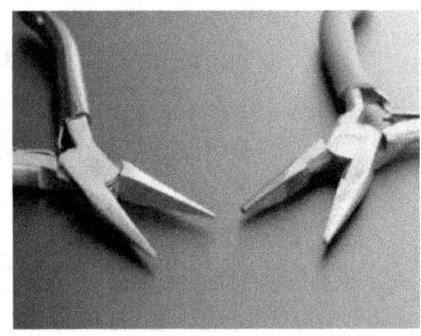

After wrapping the wire, you need to make the end of your wire flush so it looks attractive and less dangerous. Knives or scissors cannot make these cuts; hence you need to get a quality wire cutter to make your cuts. Even after making measurements and trying to cut it out, endeavor to do that with a flush cutter. It comes in various sizes and styles; choose the one most befitting to you.

Pliers

Pliers are a must in wire wrapping; you can't make certain bends and curves with just any plier. You need to use the right plier for every technique. When choosing a plier, choose the one that has a comfortable hand for you. If you have long hands, choose a long plier hand; if you have smaller hands, choose a plier with a shorter hand. Below is a list of the available pliers and their functions.

- Chain nose:

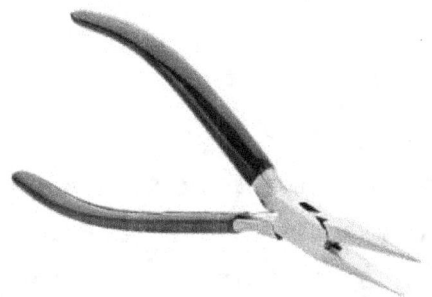

The jaws/clips are quite flat, while the outsides are rounded. This tool is tapered for use in wrapping wires, opening and clipping jump rings close. The inside is smooth and flat, making it great for straightening kinks, flattening crimp beads, and tucking wire ends. Make sure to choose a chain plier that has a small tip to help you tuck wire ends properly.

- Flat nose:

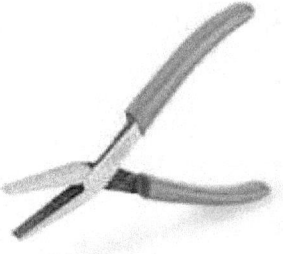

These are flat-facing clips that are used in manipulating wires. They are also called needle-nose pliers. These pliers are mostly useful in repositioning and bending wire tightly. It is mainly used for making right angles and sharp bends in a wire and other angular bends.

- Bent nose:

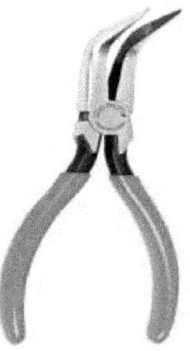

This is a plier that features gripping and snipping at wires firmly or creatively. Because of the bent shape, it allows you to work and see your object clearly without the handle getting in the way of the wire. It is also used for shaping wires and adjusting jump rings.

- Round nose:

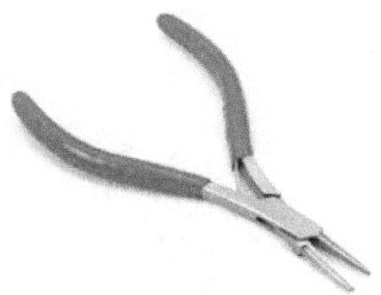

The mouth of this wire is already curved, so it makes slight curves or bends of small diameters. Round nose pliers are used in making loops, eye pins, ear wires, dangles, headpins, smooth U bends and jump rings. You can also use it in making smooth turns and swirls.

Ruler

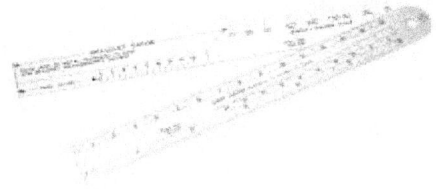

For a detailed and more intensive design, you need to take measurements of your wires. The ruler is a very important tool to help you keep a tab of your measurements and make accurate measurements whenever you want to.

Permanent Marker

After ruling out a measurement for a pair of jewelry, it is very easy to forget the number you measured when you want to make a second pair. The best thing to do is get a permanent marker to use on your wires and pliers to highlight the measurement point.

Files

Sometimes, it could be difficult to eliminate the sharp edges and you just have to trim it down. Files are necessary to help you file down every sharp edge. You can also use high sandpaper grits to smoothen the surface of a metal after hammering.

Chasing Hammer

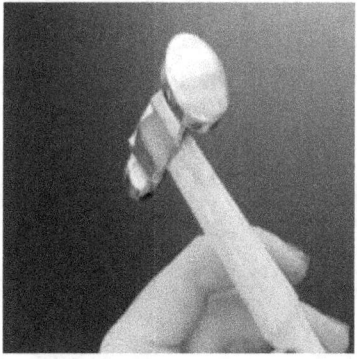

It is also called the jeweler's hammer. It has a small smooth surface and a shaped side like a peen. The smooth side is used to hammer your works to harden it and indent the metal well. You can use the other side, the peen, to smooth out dents.

Vise

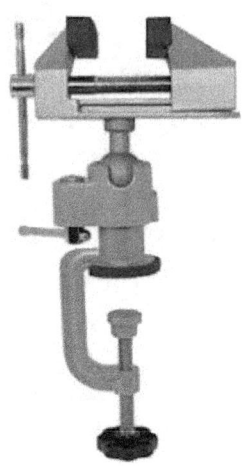

This is a tool attached to your bench or work surface. It is used for holding metals while you work on them. You can use it in holding gemstones, ear wires, mandrels, and bracelets. You can also use it to hold your jewelry while you make repairs. It is a must to use when you are working on large projects that require carefulness and precision.

Steel Bench Block

This is usually used as a second workspace while you work your jewelry. It helps to protect your main workspace from wear and tear. Also, when hammering or making use of any instrument that would require you to use the workspace, this is a great tool to use. It is best prescribed for hammering. This tool helps to reduce the shock while you hammer.

Mandrels

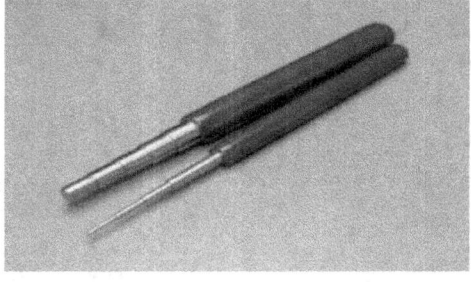

This is a shaping tool; you can use this tool to reshape metallic jewelry into any size. Mandrels are majorly used to size rings, bracelets and necklaces while you work on them. It comes in different styles and shapes to suit the shapes you intend to make and the size. You can also use it to resize existing jewelry like a ring to fit the right shape.

Metal Hole Punch

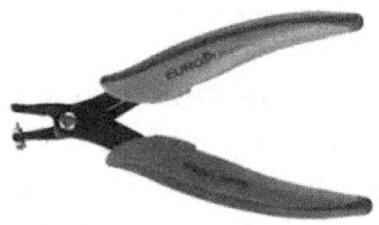

This is a tool used to punch holes into your metal while wrapping. It has a really tiny mouth inside one of its jaws. There are different hole punches for different wire gauges. The thicker the wire, the more force is needed in punching holes. Hence, you can't use the hole punch for a small wire gauge on a big gauge.

Crimp Tool

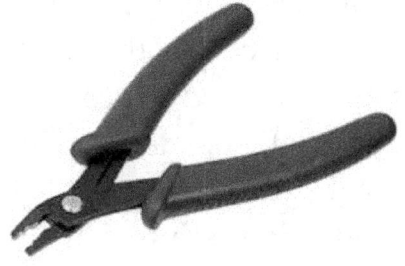

These tools are used in closing 2-3 mm crimp beads and tubes in a smooth manner. They are also used to hold wire or ends of strings firmly to prevent the design from unraveling. They help you to have a great finish at the end of your bead or bracelet so you can attach your clasp. They close crimps very attractively and efficiently.

Jigs

This is a highly brilliant tool that makes your wire wrapping easy. It helps you to create your own designs and loops with wire. You can use the jig to manipulate designs to incorporate into your jewelry production. There are different wire jig patterns; you can select as many as possible for various designs.

Setting Up Your Wire Wrapped Jewelry Studio

Before you set about building your wire-wrapped jewelry studio, you need to think about everything you'll need and the required process to get yourself to the kind of studio that you desire. This can also help you develop healthy, tidy habits like organizing materials before putting them to use. You'll need to list the tools you need to build and the process before you begin.

Here are a few questions you can ask yourself when you want to begin setting up your wire wrapped jewelry studio;

1. What area of my house can be designated as a workplace; your workshop needs to be large enough to enable you to work comfortably and store all your materials properly. If you have an extra room in the house, that's just fantastic. But if you don't have an extra room, you have to make out space. This space must not be accessible to everyone, especially if you have children at home. Also, it must be a smooth and flat surface. The space must also have handy outlets with electricity.

2. What basics am I going to need?

   1. A work surface: Practically, you need a work surface that is at least about 8 feet. Also, the walls in this area must be blank to allow you to comfortably work and work effectively.

      a. An old desk can also come in handy. If you don't have an old wooden desk, then you can use a wooden door. What is important is that you have a smooth and flat work surface that you can use at any time.

      b. One or two half-size cabinets: file cabinets are great storage options for you to store your jewelry-making materials. It also provides support as a table.

      c. A folding table

   2. Chair: a sofa is best for use as it allows you to sit for long without any form of discomfort. Asides from this, there are so many types of modern chairs that provide you great comfort. However, a chair with rollers is more comfortable because it allows you to sit for long without having to endure the pain from

putting your butts down for long. A wooden chair isn't a bad option also. Before you test the comfort before making a decision.

3. Flooring: if you want to use a carpet on your floor, you should consider putting a rubber mat under your work area. If you are working with a table, place a rubber mat under the table. This will act as protection for your carpet in case some wires drop to the floor. A rubber mat is a compulsory flooring tool, especially if you are working with gemstones and cameos. These stones can be very hard and need a cushioned floor to prevent it from causing damage when it lands to the floor.

4. Lighting: good lighting is a must if you want to have a comfortable work area. Most crafters settle for natural lightening, but this is not ideal, especially in the rainy season when the weather is unstable and the sun fails to come out often. In other words, you can't simply depend on natural lighting. A good alternative most people use is overhead fluorescent

lighting. This is a great option if it doesn't put reflect your shadow.

   a. Arm-type lamps are best for great illumination. You can place two of these on your work surface.

   b. You can use a magnifier with a helping hand to help you move the light to refocus the lens.

5. Optional work surface on your work surface: getting a second work surface on your main work surface is invaluable for the safety of your work surface and the preservation of your material. Most persons use a folded hand towel, beaders mat, a woven rubber, shelf liner that would cover the whole of your work surface area. Soft work surfaces like woven rubber do not bounce off beads or stones on the work surface. Wires do not bounce to the floor; everything stays just where you place it. Also, you can cut these materials to any size to fit your work surface area. You can also take it with it as you travel.

6. Storage: this is an indispensable necessity that you need to organize your supplies and materials. There are different types of storage systems.

   a. Small plastic: this is a common alternative. Most persons use a plastic roll-away unit with drawers that are commonly used in storing Christmas ornaments. Materials like jump rings and findings are usually kept in plastic containers or cabinets in the drawers, same with other metal tools. Small plastic is a good idea if you are just setting out and trying fresh ideas. You'll need just a few supplies. Hence, you can adopt this storage unit.

   b. Previously used containers: most crafters have found a way to use empty bottles to store their materials creatively. An unused desk or random furniture could also serve well.

   c. Filing cabinets: these storage units always come in very handy, especially when you have many materials. You can sort your wire by size, gauge size, and functions. Hence, you get to store your materials in alignment with the different descriptions and wire qualities. You can separate a drawer and label it as beads for the storing of beads and gemstones. You can also label a drawer for wires and other utilities. Depending on the number of drawers in your cabinet, you can have a drawer for every material.

    d. Television/ sound system: we all have our music types and species that tune us up. Working for a long time could be boring and quickly tiring. Music is a great tool you can use to spice up your work and reiterate your energy. You can play music from any sound system or put on a TV. Even if you are not watching it, the effect of the sounds has a way of relaxing your nerves and keep you going.

3. What to do next? You can get other tools to help make your wiring or wrapping easy and make

your personal workplace more comfortable. Some of these tools are

- A vise: this is usually used to work on long wire strands or hold your ring mandrel.
- Rotary tools
- Unique pliers
- Torches
- Battery charger for wire twister
- Plastic container to store scraps

As much as you can do without these tools, they have a way of making your work way easier. If you can afford it, don't be afraid to put it in your budget.

Wire Wrapping Jewelry Safety Precautions

Whether working at home or in the studio, you need to maintain certain safety precautions in your workshop. Wire wrapping could be harmful if not handled properly. Here is a list of 10 safety ideas for you;

- Consider your clothing: it is very essential to put on work clothes when working on a piece of jewelry. Loose sleeves and tops with long and light materials could be blown into the equipment you are working with and endanger you. Keep your hair knotted above your head or at the back

- Use safety goggles: your eyes are the jewels of your soul; you'll not want to lose them in making a jewel for your body. The best way to protect your eyes is shielding them behind a safety google.

- Wear a face mask: face masks prevent the spread of virus produced when wrapping wires on elements. The face masks will help shield you from the virus.

- Protect your fingers: to prevent scratches and wounds on your finger, you need to ensure you are well protected. Endeavor to use thick protection skins before you start working.

- Keep your workspace clear: this is important because wrapping jewelry with wire, especially if you are using chemicals. Keep away materials you are not using out of the way and put them in a storage unit to prevent accidents or dangerous spills.

- Make sure you're not working in the dark: lightning has already been highlighted as a major tool for working in your workshop. Do not work in a dark environment to prevent straining of your eyes. If you don't have good lighting, you can get a lamp to suffice or wait for the break of daylight. Working in the dark can cause you plenty of mistakes and unplanned causalities.

- Use a magnifier: to make a good wire wrapper, you need to work with a magnifier. Some elements like beads or stones could be so small that string or wiring them could be really stressful. Especially when you are working on heavy projects, you don't have the time to observe all the beads carefully before stringing. Magnifier will help to prevent you from straining your eyes, and sharpen the quality of your design.

- Use an extractor fan: ventilation is a necessity in every work environment. Even when you are the only one in the room, you still need to ensure that the room is well ventilated to prevent yourself from breathing in harmful particles produced during wiring or wrapping. An extractor fan helps to keep the environment well ventilated and free of harmful particles.

- Create a process for identifying risks: don't just go about your business absentmindedly. Be mindful of your environment, so you can quickly notice incidents of risk before they mature. When you notice potential hazards, take notes and pin them down on your notepad to secure the safety of your employees and yourself.

- Take regular breaks: when working on long-term projects, make it a practice to rest, and take periodic breaks. This will help your mind to refresh immediately. You need to be refreshed to stay motivated to work longer. When you take regular breaks, your mind is more alert and you can focus more to put in more work.

    Here is some safety equipment you need to keep close by to prevent causalities

1. PPE: this includes protective glasses, heat-proof aprons, dust masks, finger gloves and other safety clothing. You will need to get extra for yourself and everyone that will be working with you.

2. A dust extractor: if your windows don't allow for a lot of ventilation, you will need to be able to filter the air for easy and healthy breathing. Invest in buying an extractor fan for the love of your lungs.

3. A first aid kit: accidents could occur unprecedently; that's why it is called accidents. You don't plan for it, but you have to prepare for it. Keep a full first aid close by and learn how to use the contents.

4. Workspace lamps: even with the bright daylight, you want to ensure the lighting is adequate for your work and allows you to see well. Make sure every workbench has its own lamp.

Chapter 5

Wire Wrapped Jewelry Projects

Having talked about the different tools, techniques and practices in making wire wrapped jewelry, we will reveal to you 15 amazing project designs you can try out. They are all explained in very simple steps, so you can trust that after now, you'll be able to make your first ever jewelry design. Let's dive right in;

Wire Wrapped Cabochon Pendant

These pendants are so simple and beautiful. You can wear it with anything. Also, there are different templates of designs; you are restricted to following just one template. You can also customize this pendant for yourself using your creative ideas.

Tools and Supplies

- Wire; copper and bronze are good options for you if you are a beginner. It must be a nontoxic wire with a length of 5-10 feet and 21-22 gauge. The wire must also be dead soft square wire, you will need a second dead soft wire of 22 gauge, 5 feet wide and half-round. With this measurement, you can wrap a cabochon of 30-40 mm easily.
- Goldstone cabochon
- Flat nose pliers
- Round nose pliers
- Chain nose pliers
- Jewelry files
- Bail making pliers
- Wire cutters
- Ruler
- Marker

- Small round mandrel or pen

Instructions

Step 1: When making a basic wire wrap, be careful while making your initial measurement. Unroll the square wire and smoothen it with your fingers to make it straight. Ensure to straighten out every kink in the wire. Now, take your cabochon and stand it towards the tail of the wire.

Mark the spot where the wire touches the cab and roll the cab slightly around that spot. This is to ensure that the cab is sited at the circumference of the wire.

Make an additional 12 to 14 inches wire to that circumference. You will use this length of wire to make rosettes and bail. The extra wire that will be added depends on how tall you want your bail to be. If you want a really tall bail, you can add a little more than 14 inches of wire. If you are using a cheap wire, you can go an extra length and cut off the excess at the end of the project to avoid chances of wrong measurement or inadequacy.

After you have marked your measurement, make a perpendicular cut with your wire cutter. Then use this wire length as a measurement to cut the second wire.

Repeat this process until you cut four pieces of square wire. Now, make three cuts of 1 inch half round wire and one piece of 3 inches half-round wire.

Step 2: In this step, you are to make a flat strip pinned down at three different points you will use to make a tight wrap on the cab. Cut a few ½ inches of the round wire. This will be used to hold all square wires together.

Use a flat nose plier to bend the top of a one ½ round wire; the bent area should be about 3-4 mm. Then, make the bend form a simple angle. The flat side of the wire should be facing the cab. This will help the square wire to fit well.

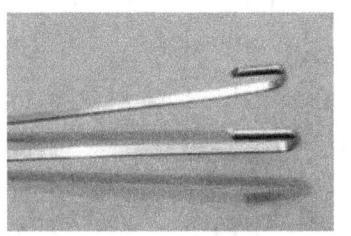 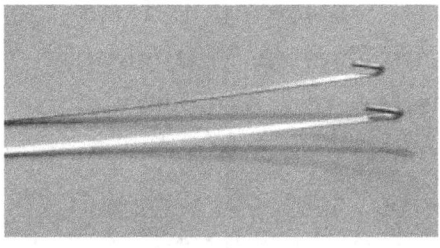

Step 3: Now, bring the square wires together in a wiggle so they are well assembled. Place a hook on the bend you created with the ½ round wire and put it over an edge. Use the flat nose plier to give it a gentle squeeze so it stays secure.

Make the front of the wraps 90 degrees to the bundle wires when wrapping. The back wraps must always be angled. Hold the square wire bundle using the flat nose plier. Position it at the point you will make the wrap with the short pieces.

Wind the ½ around the bundle; however, when turning the wire around the cab, ensure giving it a gentle squeeze using a flat nose plier. Also, you need to be prepared to move around the bundle as you wrap it with the help of the pliers.

Make a wrap around the bundle using the ½ round wire four times to end at the back of the bundle. If it exceeds the back 3-4 mm, cut to remove the excess wire.

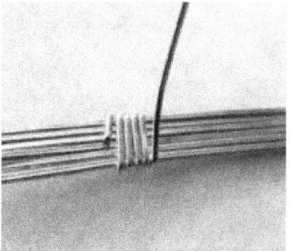
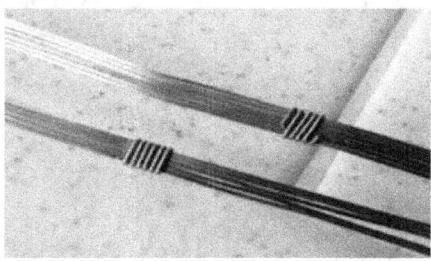

Step 4: Prepare the Bezel. Place the object on the middle point of the wrap so it is standing up. Roll it to the side till you get to one side of the cab and place a mark on the bundle. This is the point you will start the first wrap.

Measure the location of this mark to the center of the wrap. Also, mark a measurement from the wrapped center to the bundle's other side. Your second wrap will start from here. Using this direction, make 2 more wraps. Don't forget to finish wrapping on the back of the bundle.

 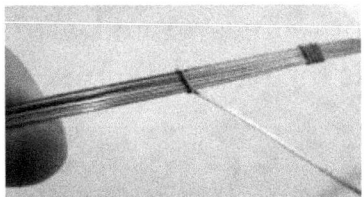

Step 5: Secure the stone. Get a small object, a bit smaller than the cab in place of a mandrel, if you don't have one. Pill bottles are a great option. Now align your bundle of wire to rest against your mandrel, using your thumb to press the center wrap.

Make the bottle perpendicular to the mandrel. Afterward, carefully adjust the sides so that they touch slightly. Now, take away the mandrel and try it on your cab. Let your fingers smooth it in properly.

The wrap is to be positioned directly under the cab. Now push the wires so it rests well on the body of the cab, and it all gets to the top and touches each other. However, the bead doesn't need to come too close so they don't tangle.

Next, get a 3 inches half-round wire and bend it slightly at the top, don't make an angel with it. Join and hook this bend to the bezel's back, and secure tightly using your pliers. Wind the top wires together using your fingers.

Make this wind at least five times. Now cut out the extra wire, don't cut too close, so you can bend the little remaining wire to the back wires using the round pliers.

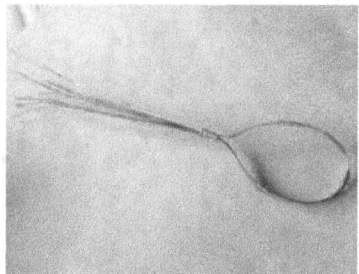

Step 6: Set the stone. Set your bezel so it is sited around the cab, and place it on the table. Pull out the outermost wires over the cab on the front side and the back side.

With your fingers, you can separate the wires and tighten them with a round nose plier. There are usually four sections of wire between the bundle. Pull the main center wire with your finger so it comes to the center. Do this on all four sections and turn the cab over to repeat the process.

Note your cab should not be held tightly. Slightly twist the front section of the pulled wire that is below using your plier, repeat this exercise with the next wire, and the upper wires. This will ensure the wires are tighter. Twist these wires that are pulled out at the back more firmly to secure your cab in a bezel.

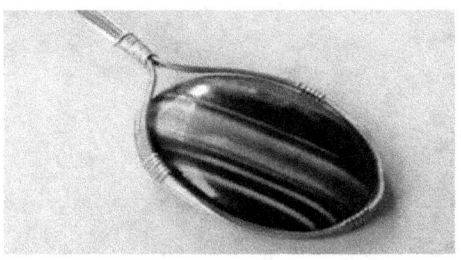 

Step 7: Make a bail. The bail is the top part of the pendant that is hanging from the top of the chain and this can be made into different sizes. Pliers of different

sizes can be used to make a bail, however, you can likewise use a fat knitting needle or a pen.

Separate the top wires with your fingers so you can identify the four wires at the front. You'll use this in making your bail. Bend the back wires slightly so it comes down at the sides. Then get a mandrel and put it just inside the bail wires, above the joined part. Then adjust the wires so it is bent over the pen, do not allow it overlap. Position the mandrel in a suitable place then, wind a piece from the back wires around the bail wires, leaving the bail wires to the security of the stem.

Allow the pen to remain in the bail so that it stays till the wires are totally finished.

 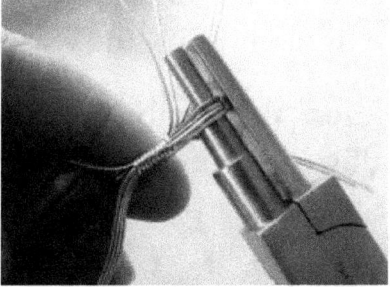

Step 8: Finish the loose wires.

Making a filigree: this requires real artistry. Filigree is a delicate-looking swirl and swoop that makes the entire design of the wire wrap. The loose wires left after the cab has been set is usually used with the following techniques;

Rosettes: this is an exciting and familiar design element amongst wire wrapping techniques. Making a rosette is simple when using the round nose plier to create a tiny loop at the tail of the wire. Wound the loop into a really tight spiral using flat-nosed pliers. Firmly grip the wire with one hand and move the wire in a rotational form a turn like the quarter at one time. Make the rosettes using twisted and untwisted wire to get different unique looks.

Loops: make loops and unique shapes with the wire. This can grow into a whole lot of fun. However, don't make it too big or the wire could bend easily. Swoop the wire tight and find the way to secure a wire's end.

Bundles: for a more serious look, make a bundle by putting different loose wires and wrapping it with a half-round wire. Make loops or tuck to finish the ends in the bezel.

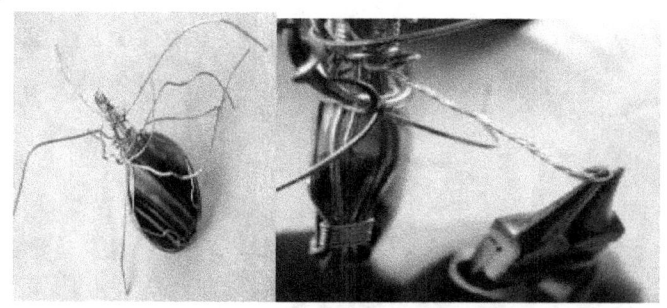

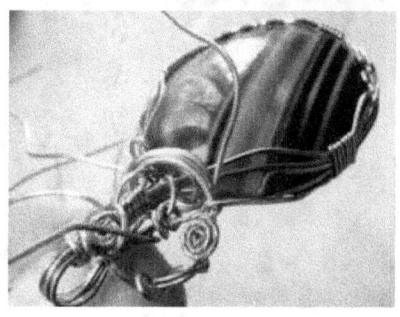

Step 9: All done. Now that you are done, to give your work a perfect finish, trim off the excess wire and dispose of them or have them stored properly for other future projects. That is, if the wire is of a sizeable length. Also, after trimming, don't forget to tuck every loose end under. Check for rough spots on the pendant using your fingers. Rub your fingers through the pendant; you can also use a piece of fabric to rub the pendant. File and trim every exposed wire or spot that you see until that surface is perfect and smooth. Now, you can add a patina, buff, and/or seal your pendant if you

want. When your finishes are dry, you can now put a cord or chain in your pendant.

Wire Wrapped Bead Rings

This is an interesting project idea, especially if you are a lover of rings. You don't need so many materials and supplies to make this ring. As a beginner, you are sure to fall finish off this project in no time.

Tools and Supplies

- Beads
- 20 Gauge silver-plated copper wire
- Ring sizer
- Wire cutters
- Jewelry plier

Instructions

Step 1: Cut 12-14 inches of wire. Place the bead at the center and bend two sides of the slightly so the bead doesn't go anywhere. Put the bead in your ring sizer groove, and wrap the ends of the wire around the mandrel one time. This is just a fancy word for the ring sizer. The size of the area you will wrap needs to be considered because the wrapping tends to get tighter as you work. Hence, make your size half larger than the size you are planning to make. 7 is a general size if you are short of the size to use.

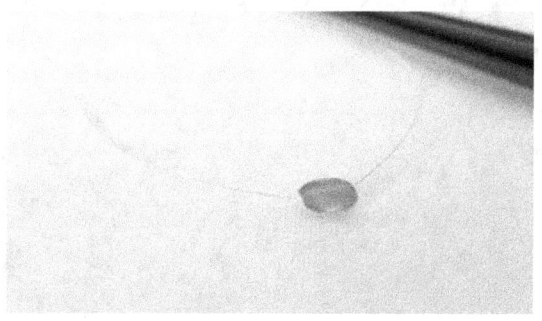

Step 2: Wrap the end of the wire around a mandrel and bend it around the bead. Your work has taken a form, so you can take it from the mandrel to work on it. Separate the wire ends and make a wrap with them around the bead. Make sure to work in a counter-clockwise fashion. This way, you get to wrap both wires in the same direction.

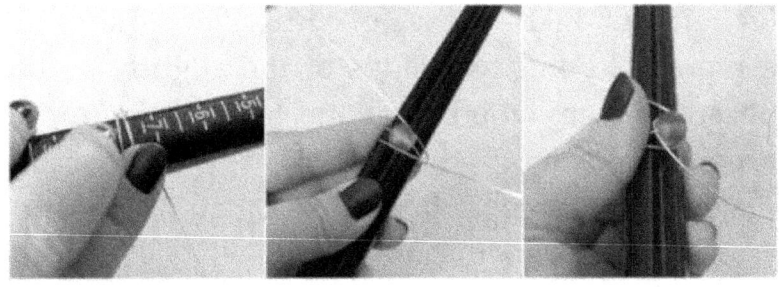

Step 3: At the end, you will definitely have a few inches of wire left; wrap it around the base of the ring 3-4 times using pliers. Cut off the excesses thereafter. Ensure to file the end of the wire. You can use a ring sizer to work out any bent area.

Step 4: Thereafter, smoothen the wire rings down to press the wires back together. Then form it into a round shape. You might have a little trouble if you are trying a wrapped wire ring for the first time. However, with more trials, you are sure to amaze yourself.

Making smaller wrapped wire rings have different and more difficult procedures, especially because you are wrapping smaller rings, which means you have a smaller area to work on. Hence start working big like you did in the big rings but be mindful of working your rings down. You'll most certainly fall in love with this ring unlike anything you'd get in the store

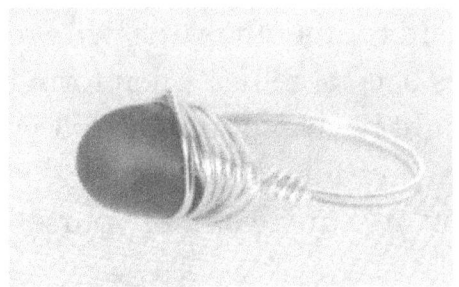

Wire Wrapped Bead Bracelet

This is one of the simplest projects you would ever try as a beginner. Here are tools and materials needed to start;

Tools and Supplies

- Beads; color beads matching the color of your wire.
- A closure

- Colored wire matching the color of your beads
- Pliers
- Yarn

Instructions

Step 1: Get a length of wire and bend the tip as shown in the picture. Now use a plier to bend it backward. The first bend helps you to lock the wire and the bead, the second bend enables you to commence the wrapping process. Add this wire to the bead to wrap it off. After wrapping, cut off the excess wire carefully.

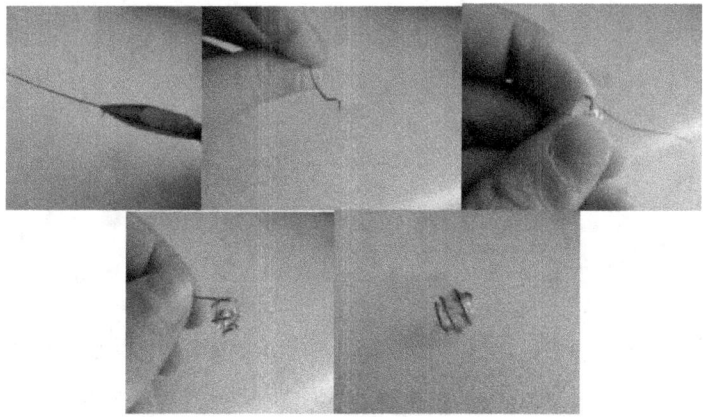

Step 2: Wrap all the beads you intend to use until you are sure they are enough.

Step 3: Now, add all the wrapped beads to the yarn. When putting the yarn, put it through the place where you started wrapping your beads. Also, to make your work faster, thicken the tip of the yarn using thickeners like nail polish.

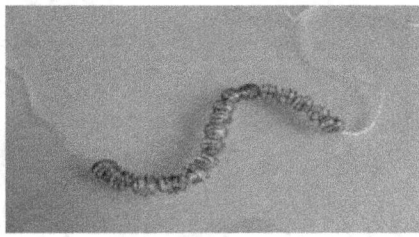

Step 4: After you have added all the beads into the yarn, carefully add your closure. Knot your yarn twice, then tie it together. Afterward, coil a piece of wire around the closure point and cut off the unneeded yarn. Do these for the other part of the closure.

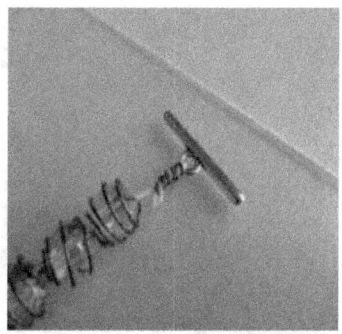

Step 5: Your project is as good as finished after you add your closure. You can produce as many bracelets as possible.

Wire Wrapped Bead Earrings

Many crafters happen to approve of this project as a great option, especially as a beginner. It will sharpen your skill of manipulating wire with your hands and pliers. You will also learn how to shape wire using a bench block and hammer. You will also learn to open and close jump rings to attach your beads to ear wires.

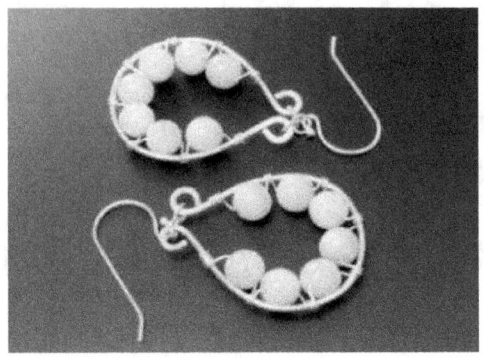

Tools and Supplies

- 6mm round beads
- Flush cutters/Smooth jaw pliers
- Flat-nosed pliers
- Round nose pliers
- Chasing hammer or a bench block
- Ear wires
- Small ruler
- Jump rings
- Safety glasses
- Silver-plated wire: depending on the type of earring you want to make, you will need a wire of about 4 inches with a larger gauge wire. This is almost an arm's length of the wrapping wire. This wire is silver in color and can be used to make several experiments. When selecting a wire for

ear rings, you need to find certain wires that won't affect the sensitivity of people's skin. Sterling silver ear wires are a great recommendation.

Instructions

Step 1: Cut and curl wires. Straighten your heavier wire using flat-nosed pliers or wrap it with a mallet on a smooth work surface. Measure and cut two 4 inches' pieces of wire, and cut with a flush snip. Note that the length of the wire is equal to the length of the earring. Make sure the two lengths of the two wires are the same and match evenly. When you cut with the flush cutter, it could produce a less pointy wire, so you would have to trim the wire to ensure the ends are flat.

Now take the round nose pliers to firmly hold the end of your wires, then twist it around to form a loop. Ensure that the wire closes to reach itself; if it doesn't, apply more pressure to tighten the gap. Afterward, flatten the loop with a chasing hammer or a bench block by hitting it seven good times. Flip the loop to the other side and do the same. This way, both sides will look flat. Asides from the flat appearance of the wire, the texture of the wire is also changed. It is firmer than it used to be. Hammering gives it a much stronger shape and appearance.

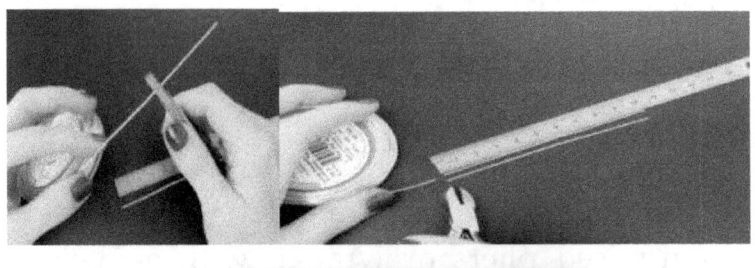

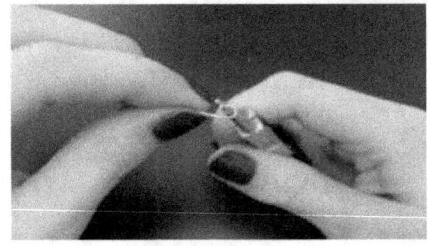

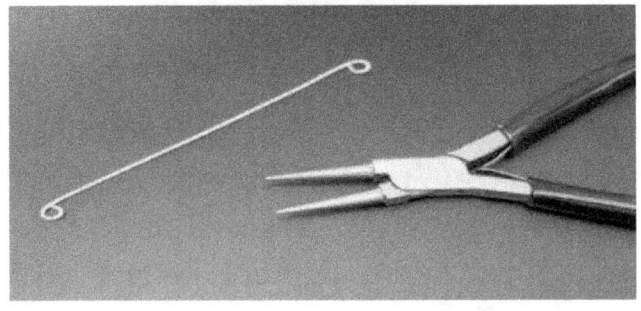

Step 2: String beads and begin wrap. Shapen your wire to a teardrop shape using your fingers and pliers. Use your hammer's handle with any round object to readjust your shape. Don't trouble yourself trying to make it look just as perfect as the image in this step. The

most important aim of this step is that your earrings are matching.

Now, you are to work in your bead wire. String seven beads into the thinner wrapping wire and bend one end into a kink to prevent losing the beads. The unkinked wire should be laid across the teardrop shape and wrapped about it six times using a plier. Make the wrap counterclockwise, so it is tighter. You must make the wrap in the same direction throughout the wrap. Wrap the wire ends towards the largest loop. Hence, the body of the earring doesn't have to cross over the loops on its way around. Snip the excess wire off, and squeeze in the cut end with a plier so there is a smooth finish at the ends.

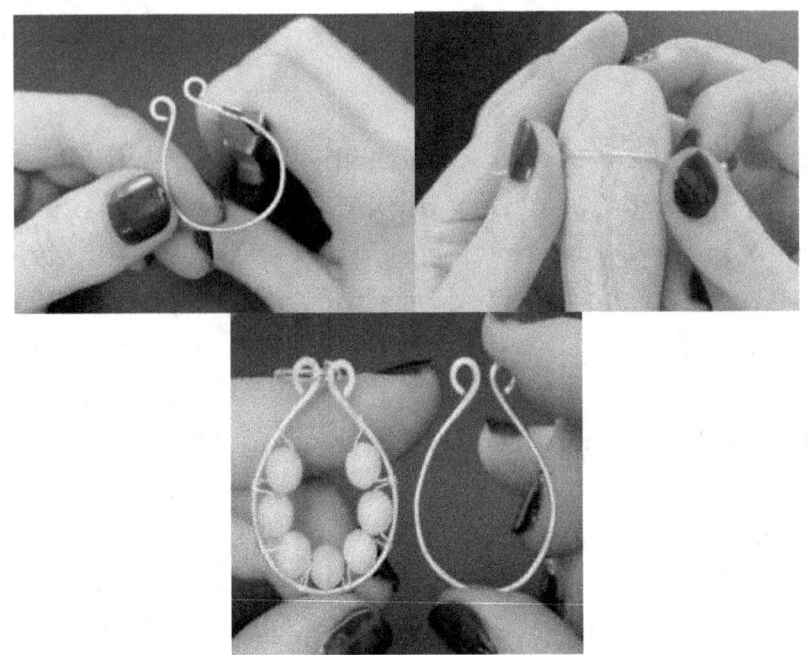

Step 3: Incorporate beads. Incorporating the beads can be quite a stress if you are doing it for the first time. Push a bead down the wire so it is close to the larger wire loop. Place a firm hold with one hand on the loop. Wrap the wire around the large wire twice and reposition the slack so that it dodges the end of the wire. Slide another bead down its wire and begin the same wrapping process.

As you incorporate the beads, make sure that the spacing is even and your wires are snugged. If there is any unevenness that you notice, adjust it with the flat-nosed pliers and pinch them close to each other.

Complete this process by adding seven beads to the earring. You would have some remaining wire, wrap it around the earring six times, then trim and pinch the tail as you did earlier. This step is basically a repetition of adding beads into the wire loop and wrapping it twice to go around the larger wire. If yours doesn't look perfect, you can have a second try.

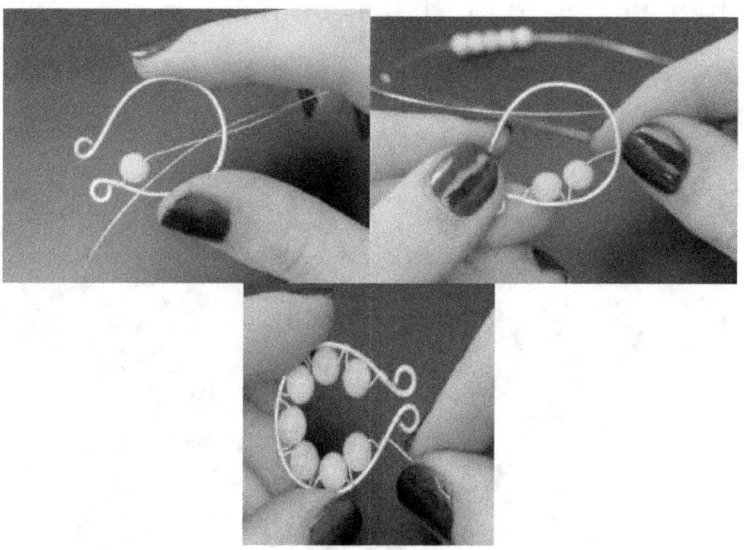

Step 4: Finish up with jump rings. Use jump rings to connect your ear wires. Jump rings are majorly smallish loops of wire with a small opening. Although

there are several sizes of jump rings and other shapes, ensure to use a size suitable for you and your project. Twist open the jump rings with your fingers, loop one end into your masterpiece at the tail, and close it up by twisting it back.

Repeat the same process and connect the other end of your masterpiece with a jump ring. Now, loop the two ends together with a third jump ring. Now attach the ear wire into the jump rings. Repeat this process with the other earring to make it a complete pair.

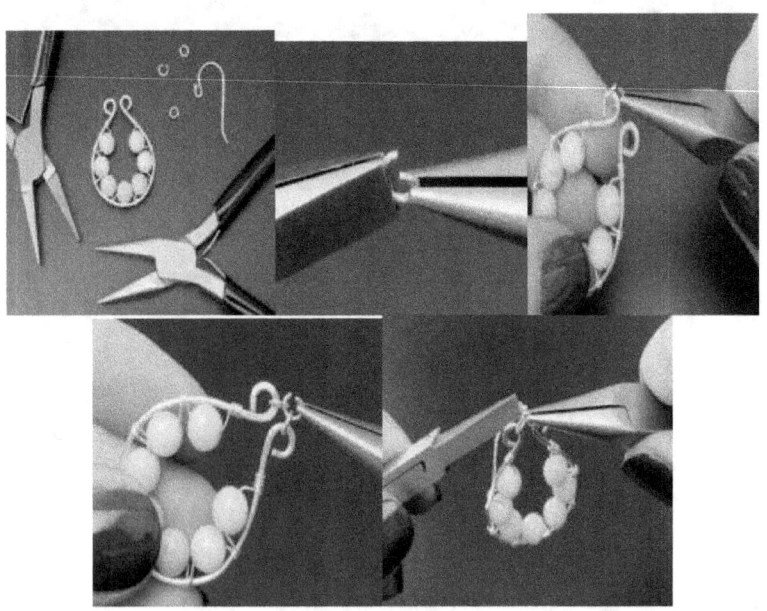

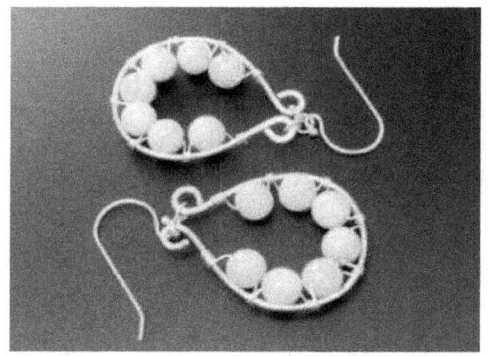

Crystal Wrapped Cuff Bracelet

This is just as interesting to make as it looks. In less than an hour, you can make one of these beauties. If you are such a jewelry person, you can invest more time and resources in making more. The supplies listed here are to help you make one cuff bracelet.

Tools and Supplies

- 2 inches of 24-gauge gold wire

- 4.5 inches of Rhinestone chain
- One hammered Cuff Bracelet
- One pair needle nose pliers
- One pair Shear Flush Cutters

Instructions

Step 1: Create a bend of 90 degrees on the end of the 24-gauge gold wire. Pick the hammered cuff bracelet and wrap the wire around the backside of the cuff ¾ inches from the end. Wrap the wire three times around the cuff. Wrap tightly so the wire is secured to the cuff. Then tug firmly at the wire using a needle nose plier. Use your flush cutters to trim off the excess wire.

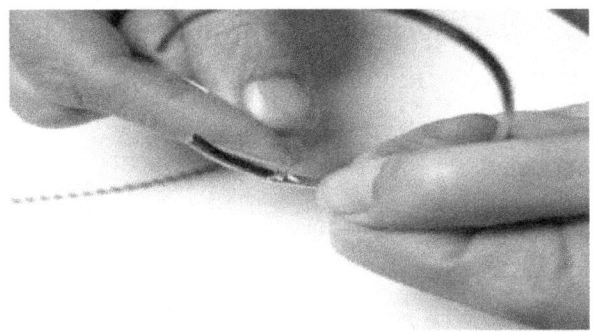

Step 2: Place the rhinestone chain on the cuff so one end of the rhinestone is close to the starting point of the wrap. Hold the rhinestone chain firmly in the right

position and make two wraps after the first gap of the chain.

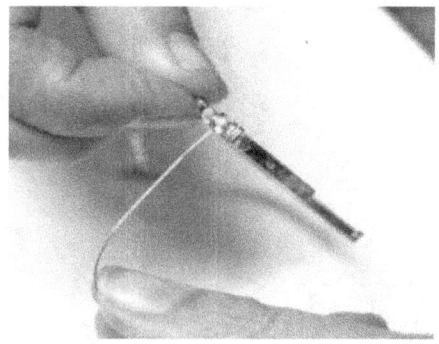

Step 3: From that point, make two wraps in the next gap of the rhinestone chain. Continue making two wraps in every gap until you get to the other end of the bracelet. Stop the wrap at ¾ inches from the end.

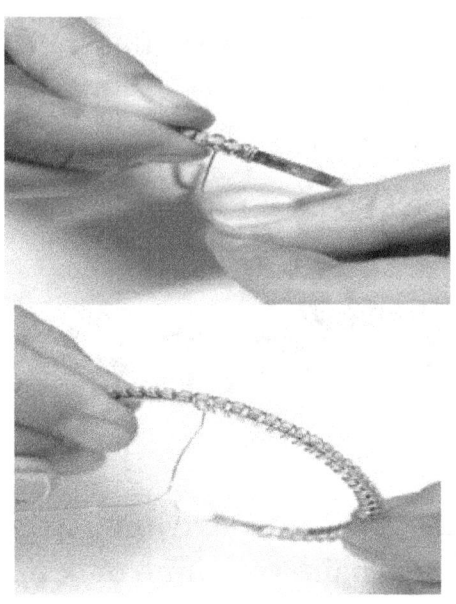

Step 4: At this point, wrap the wire in between the gap of the chain twice; make sure it is very tight so your rhinestone chain doesn't fall out afterward. After that, cut off the excess chain with your flush cutter.

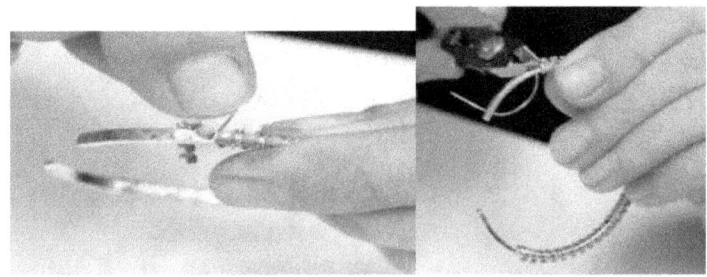

Step 5: After you cut the excess rhinestone, wrap your wire on the last link two more times. Turn over your

bracelet and tuck your wire so it is bent well and doesn't pose any danger to you. Use a needle nose plier to pick the wires and pull it tightly, so it is firm on the bracelet, and bend it in. use flush cutters to cut off the excess wire. Do this on the other side of the bracelet where you started wrapping from. Your bracelet is ready. You can follow this step to make as many bracelets as possible.

Beaded Wire Heart Necklace

This technique is very versatile and you can achieve an awesome result with any type of bead that fits or matches your wire.

Tools and Supplies

- 18g heart wireframe (it should come with a swirl at the bottom so you can hang a bead there)
- Crochet hook
- Thinner wire for attaching the beads
- Beads

Instructions

Step 1: Wrap the wire around the frame three times to secure your wire to the frame. Don't bother about your wraps being loose when you start; smoosh it along the line to make it tighter.

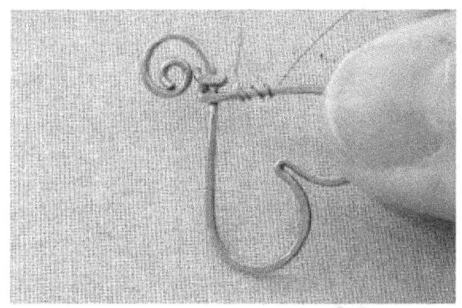

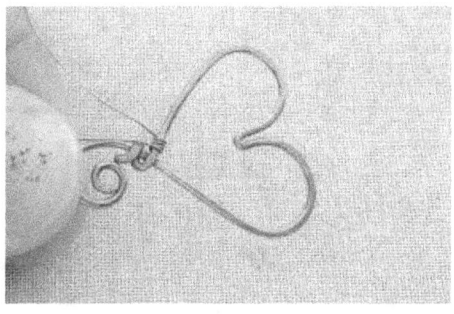

Step 2: You can start adding your beads into the wire. Add the first bead, and adjust it tightly. Then pull the wire through the frame, and wrap the frame again to ensure the bead is secured in that position. You can use a crochet hook to help you grab the wire when passing it through the frame.

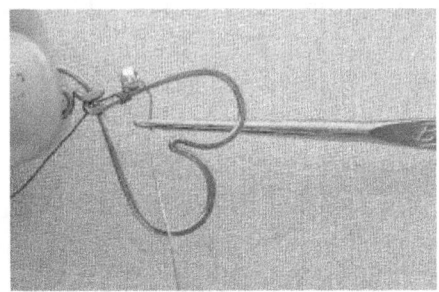

Step 3: Repeat the process and add more beads. Make a wrap through the frame after adding every bead. Because of the shape of the frame, your beads may start to lose position as you continue wrapping; you might need to use something really firm to keep the beads in position or keep turning the beads.

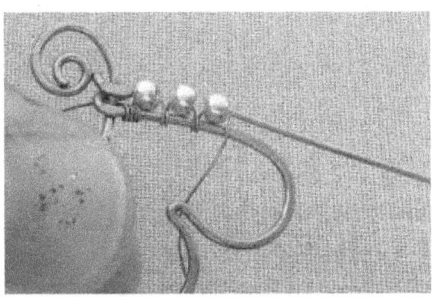

Step 4: The middle of the heart can be quite tricky. But just make extra wraps at that middle point to create a wire bridge for you to add your jump ring to join with your pendant. Then continue wrapping till the end of the frame. Make at least three tight wraps to secure your beads at the end firmly. Trim the remaining wire

off and lay it flat using your plier. To check how flat it is, rub your hands over it and ensure it won't tamper with the skin or clothes.

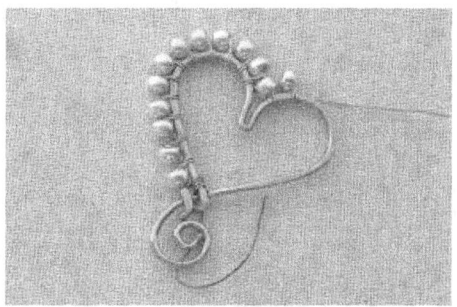

Step 5: Add a jump ring to the middle of the heart; your pendant is ready. You can add it to any chain you wish. If you want to attach a silver dangle as shown in this picture at the tail of the heart, then use a headpin.

Crescent Moon Wire Wrapped Necklace

This would mean something special to you if you are a lover of signs and symbols. You can use any color of wire and beads you choose. The wire type and bead type are also up to you.

Tools and Supplies

- 0.8mm wire for the frame
- 0.4mm wire to wrap the beads
- Jump ring and golden necklace
- Small beads of 3mm and 4mm (preferably Czech glass)
- Seed beads of sizes 11 and 8
- Cutters, round nose pliers, and chain nose pliers
- Marker pen

Instructions

Step 1: Measure the 0.8mm wire and cut out a length of 12 inches. Now use your wire marker pen to mark the middle of the 12 inches wire. Then bend from that point to form a teardrop shape.

Step 2: Adjust your shape to be 1 ¼ inch across.

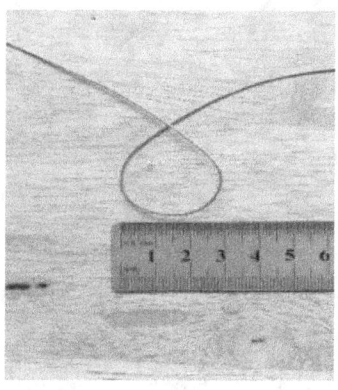

Step 3: Make a wrapped loop by bending one of the wires straight up with your round nose pliers.

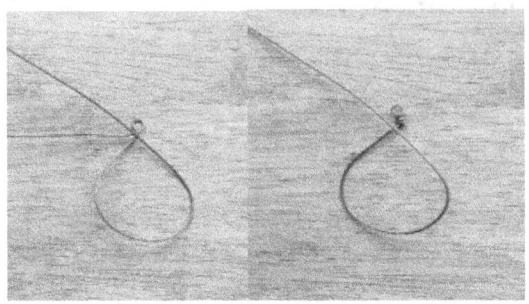

Step 4: Hold both wires with your chain nose plier at the top of the teardrop shape, just as in the picture. Then wrap the existing wraps a little before cutting off excess wire.

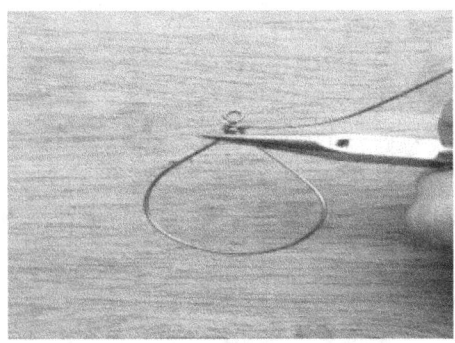

Step 5: Hold the wire using chain nose pliers at the point indicated with a red arrow, and bend your teardrop slightly to turn it into a crescent moon

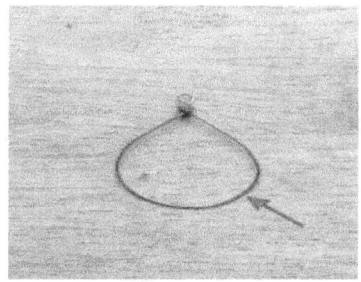

Step 6: Using the chain-nose pliers to bend the wire back in the shorter section. Adjust it a little with your hands so it looks less like a banana.

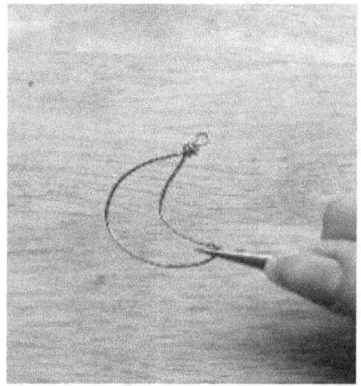

Step 7: Pick your small bead and wire of 0.4 mm, wrap the end of your crescent near the loop, and cut off the excess wire, appearing as a short tail.

Step 8: Put in 2 to 3 beads in the wire and wrap it on the crescent to make it secure.

Step 9: You can thread in 2, 3 beads in a sequence and wrapping the wire after threading in.

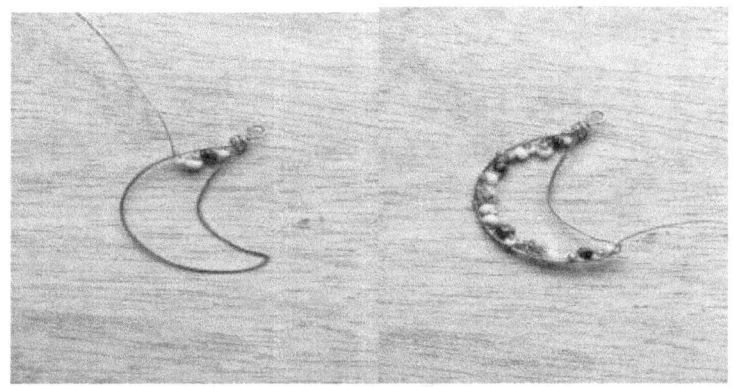

Step 10: Continue wrapping until you cover the whole crescent with beads. After that, wrap the crescent tightly before cutting off the excess.

Step 11: Use a jump ring to join the pendant to the necklace. Your pendant is ready to wear.

Folded Wired Ring

This is one of the easiest projects you can ever try. If you haven't worn these types of ring, you will get to realize how comfortable and adjustable these rings are after making them. They are perfectly awesome.

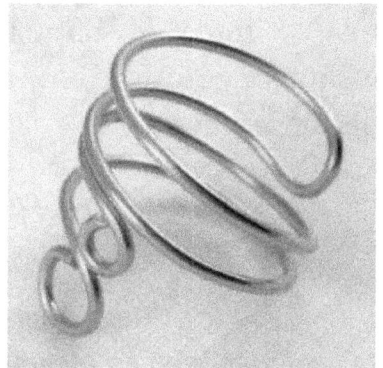

Tools and Supplies

- Ruler
- Wire-cutter
- Round nose plier
- Chain nose plier
- Ring mandrel
- Nylon or rawhide hammer
- 7 to 10 inches of 18-gauge round wire (copper or brass)

Instructions

There are three major ways to fold your wire;

Method 1 – The flat fold: You will achieve a compact double ring shank with this method.

Firstly, bend your wire into a U shape using the round-nose pliers. Then squash your fold, so it is perfectly flat-sung under the flat nose plier.

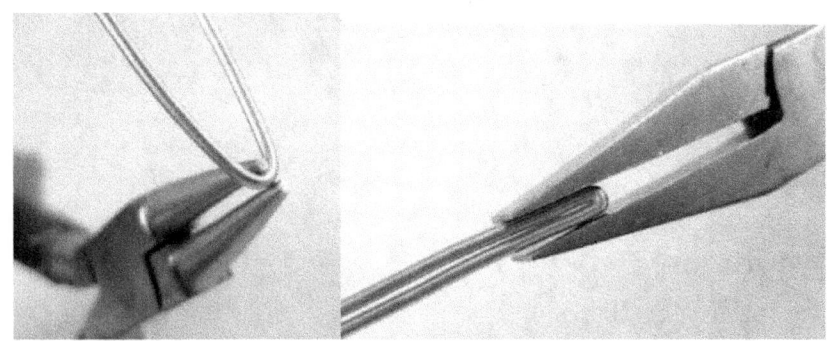

Thereafter, wrap the flat folded wire on the ring mandrel. Pound the shank with your hammer into a very good ring shape. Start hammering from the folded end, then move to the point where your wires meet with the fold.

You can remove the wire from the mandrel; this is what you will have thereafter. You have two long wire ends that you are to use in manifesting your artistic ideas.

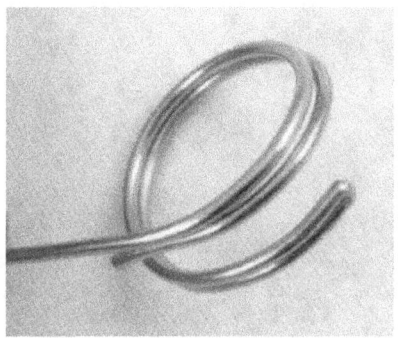

You can make spirals with the round nose plier and a simple curl to have something like the image above. Then put the ring back into the mandrel for finishing. Hammer the wire lightly to ensure that the design curves naturally over the wearer's finger, as well as make your ring sturdy and your design firmer.

An alternative to this design, still under the flat fold method, is this; after making the flat fold, separate the two other ends so that it straddles the end. This way, the flat fold comes in the middle of the ring and the straddles; you can make these straddles with the round nose plier.

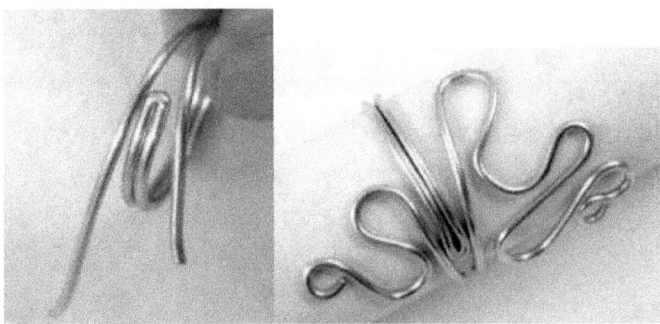

Method 2 – The round fold: This method gives you an open work double ring shank. However, the process is faster; all you need to do to get the round fold is bend the piece of wire into a U shape using the round nose plier.

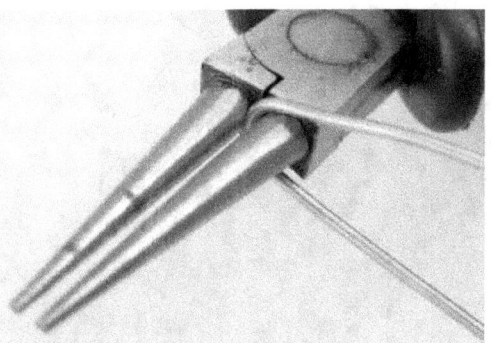

Afterward, wrap the wire around the mandrel. Then hammer only the shank portion in the wire; hammering the whole wire can harden the wire and make further adjustments hard. You can wrap it straddle style round the mandrel like in the image, using the long wire ends to straddle the round fold.

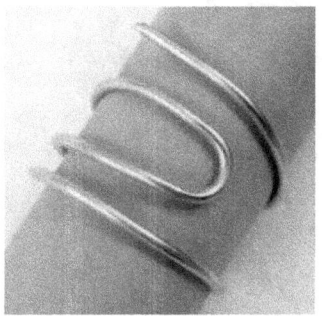

You can also wrap spiral style to have something like this;

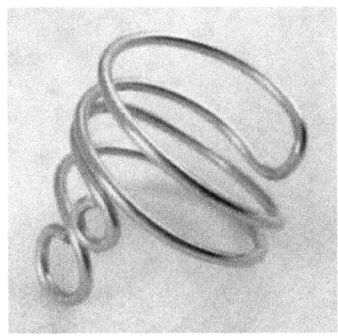

Method 3 – The square fold: This gives an angular look to your ring. Shape the end of your two long wire ends into swirls and sweet curls; you will have very nice curves. This method is mainly used in making masculine ring designs. Bend your long wire with flat nose pliers into a U shape.

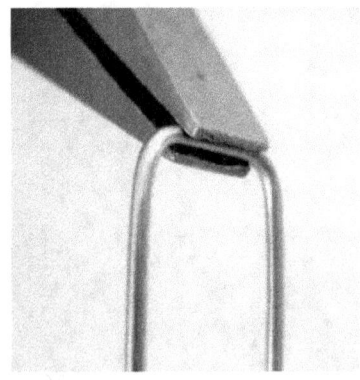

Afterwards, wrap the wire on the mandrel in straddle style. Hammer the shank portion of your wire so it is firm. The angles of the ring are in contrast to spirals.

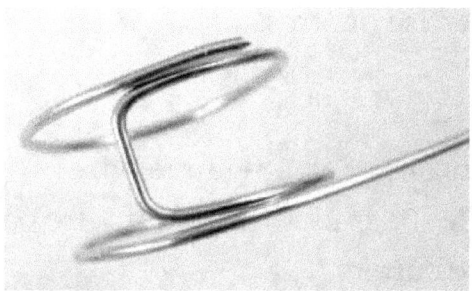

The result is more amazing if your two wire ends are of different lengths. In the end, you can put extra elements to your wire rings like beads, patina effects and other jewelry techniques to make your design outstanding.

Zen Wired Spiral Pendant

You might have seen this somewhere; it is very simple and looks super amazing. Again, it doesn't require much expertise or stress.

Tools and Supplies

- 10 inches of an 18-gauge wire
- A file for smoothening off wire ends
- Wire cutters
- Round nose pliers
- Jewelry hammer
- Steel jeweler's block

Instructions

Step 1: Measure and cut out your 10 inches wire. Smoothen the ends with a file.

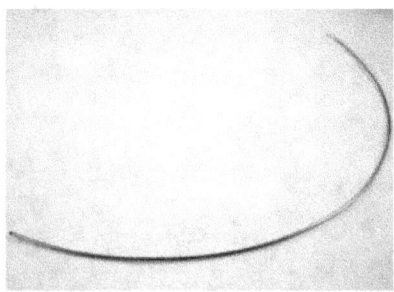

Step 2: Make a nice pendant bail using your round-nose pliers. You might want to make them big so they can fit into any cord or chain size.

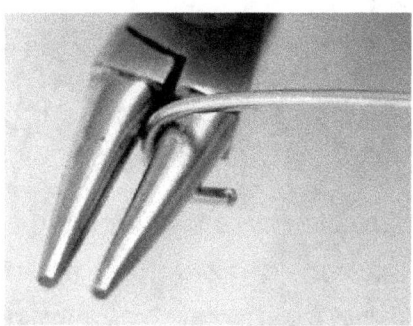

Step 3: Make a big circle on the end where you made the bail with the fat end of your round nose plier.

Step 4: Make more circles by moving our plier round the wire three or four more times. You will end up with something like this

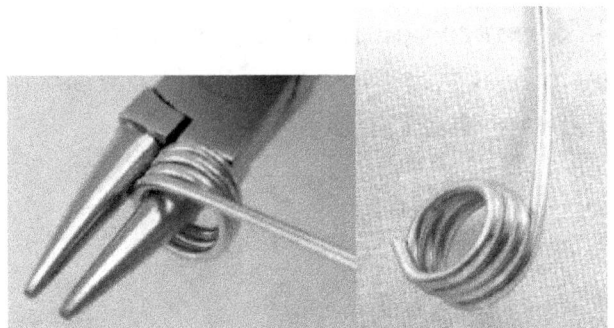

Step 5: Make a simple spiral at the other end of the wire with the pliers. Move your pliers along the wire slightly as you curve your wire into an open spiral.

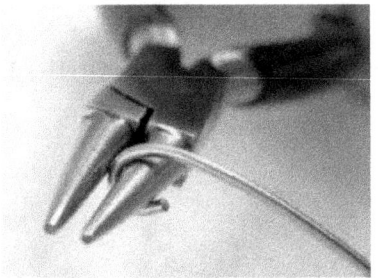

Step 6: Continue spiraling until you get the top of the bail.

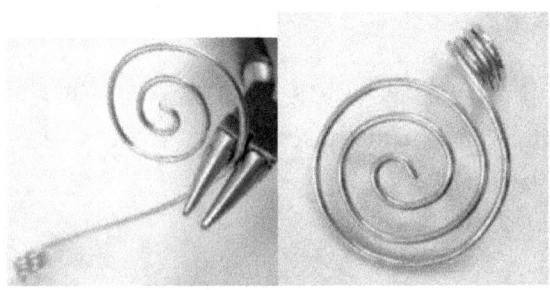

Step 7: Bend the bail using the tips of your round nose plier until it is perpendicular to the spiral.

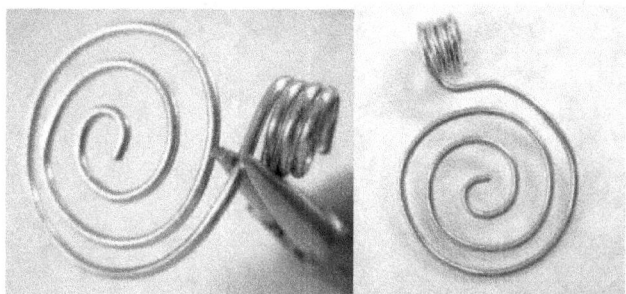

Step 8: Hammer the wire on a steel jeweler's block to get your pendant ready for wear. Hammer with the flat side to harden the metal, then you can use the peen to hammer the wire softly to create little dents in the metal.

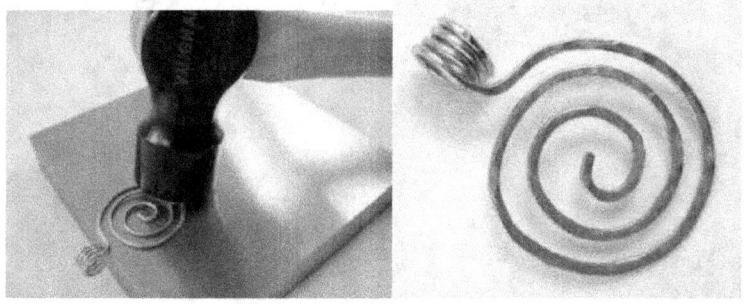

I love them best on a leather or suede cord

Birch Leaf Wired Earrings

You might want to use really attractive colors to make this project. Although this project looks a little complex, it only requires precision and carefulness. It is not much different from other projects that have been explained earlier.

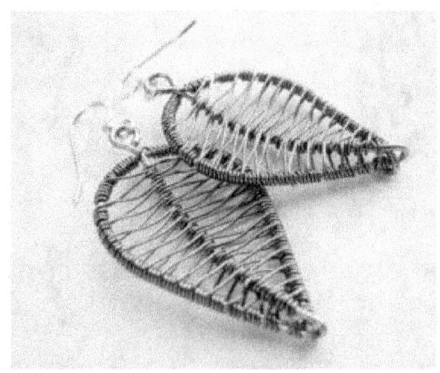

Tool and Supplies

- Round dowel
- Wire cutters
- Round nose pliers
- Chain nose pliers
- One pair of ear wires
- 30 cm of 18 gauge round dead soft wire
- 2.4 meters of 26 gauge round dead soft wires

Instructions

Step 1: The frame is quite simple. You can make it in few minutes. Pick your 18-gauge wire and curve one-third of the wire around the dowel like in the picture, so the wire crosses itself slightly.

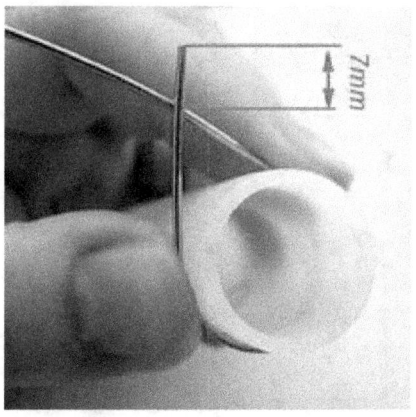

Step 2: Repeat step one to have a matching pair of leaves

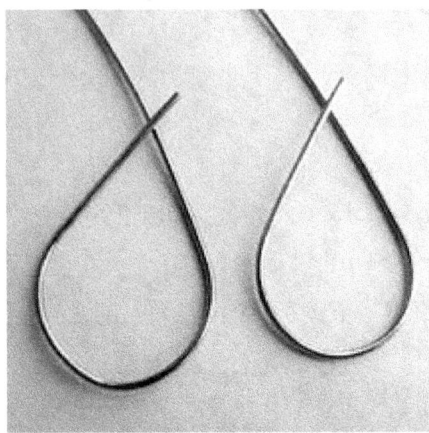

Step 3: Join the wires firmly together at the point where they overlap using the round nose plier, then bend the long wire over the forming frame to touch the joining point at the middle. You will use this in making the central vein of the leaf.

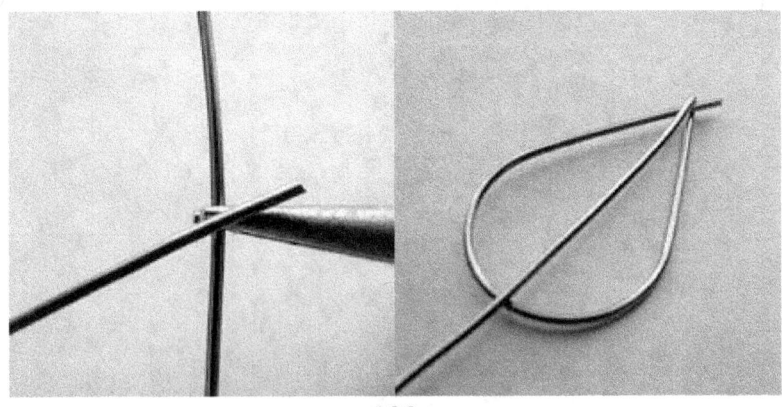

Step 4: Get your 26-gauge wire; this will be used as your wrapping wire. Give a few inches to the tail of the leaf, and start wrapping the side of the frame with a long wire.

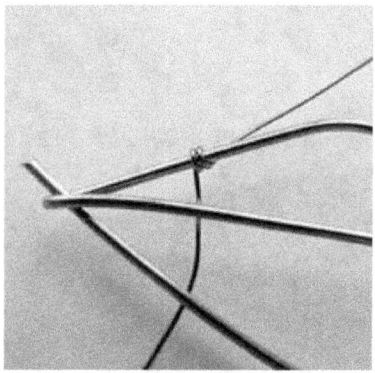

Step 5: Adjust the wrap by pushing it up to the corner of the frame. Then wrap the wire over the middle wire or the center vein.

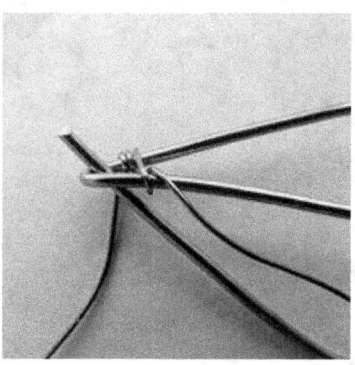

Step 6: Pass the wire under the short wire and wrap it as the arrow points. Wrap it so that the wire is pressed close to the frame.

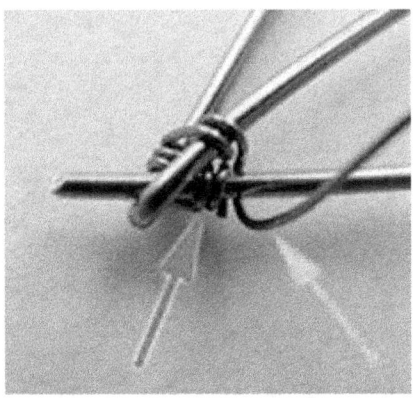

Step 7: Use the wire in wrapping the short wire twice

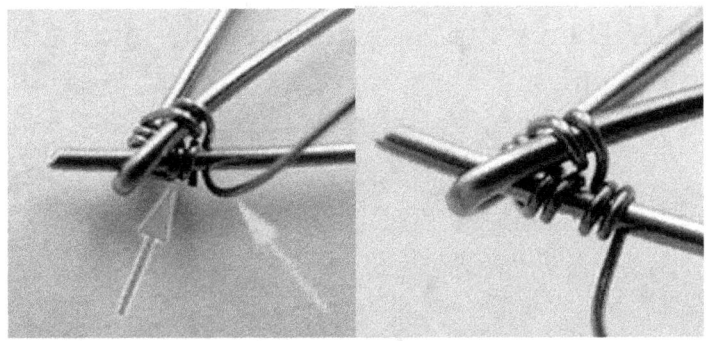

Step 8: Wrap the middle wire or middle vein once before moving to the other wire.

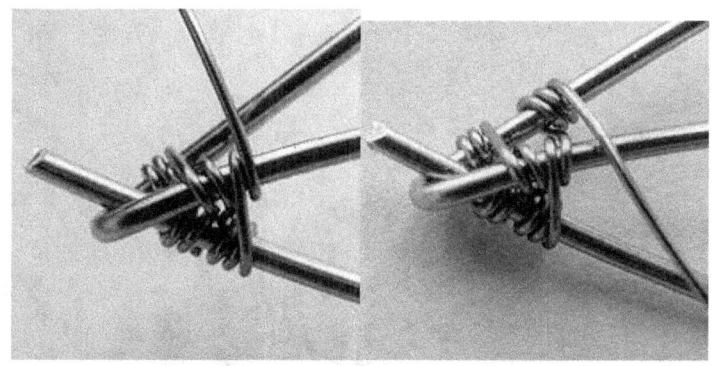

Step 9: Wrap the wire around the frame twice as you did in step 7

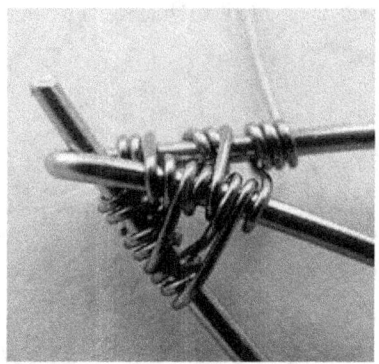

Step 10: Increase your wraps to five as you get close to the end of the frame on each side.

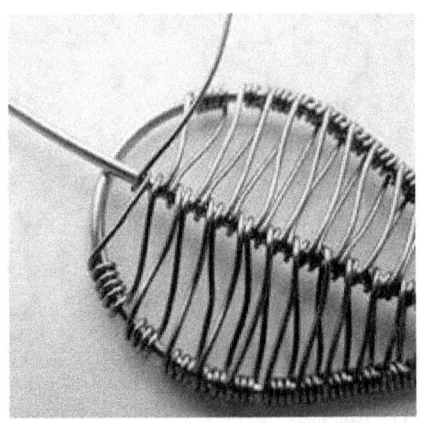

Step 11: Once you have successfully wrapped the sides of the frame, wrap the midrib finally, tuck and trim

Step 12: Bend the tail of the short wire at the top of the frame with a plier, tuck it slightly at a corner.

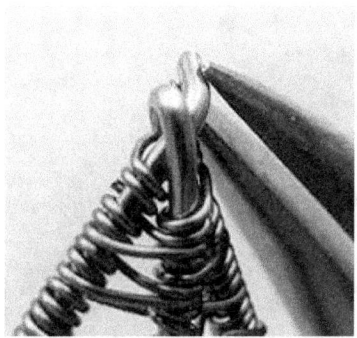

Step 13: You can press the frame slightly to create a curve. This is optional, though.

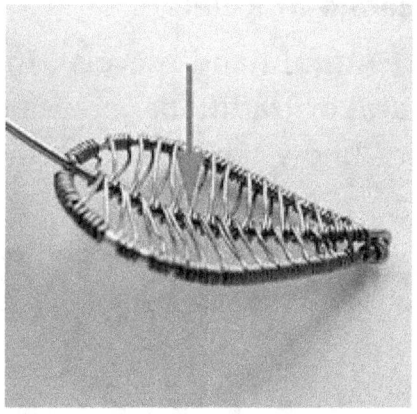

Step 14: Make a loop with the remaining midrib to attach your ear wire.

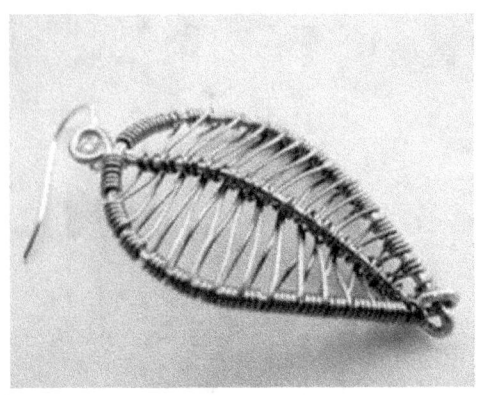

Wire Bangle Beaded Bracelets

This is a very beautiful hand bracelet. In most places, it is used for cultural or traditional occasions. However, it is so lovely that I know you wouldn't mind having one of these.

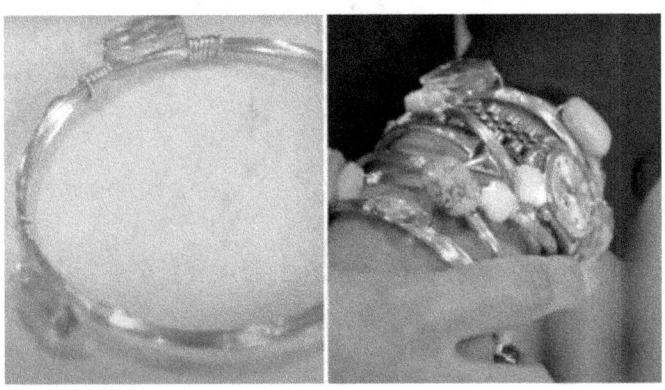

Tools and Supplies

- Wire cutters
- Beads of your choice
- Soda
- 20 gauge gold wire

Instructions

Step 1: Prepare your supplies and make sure that there are as close as they can be. 10 feet of wire is a good start.

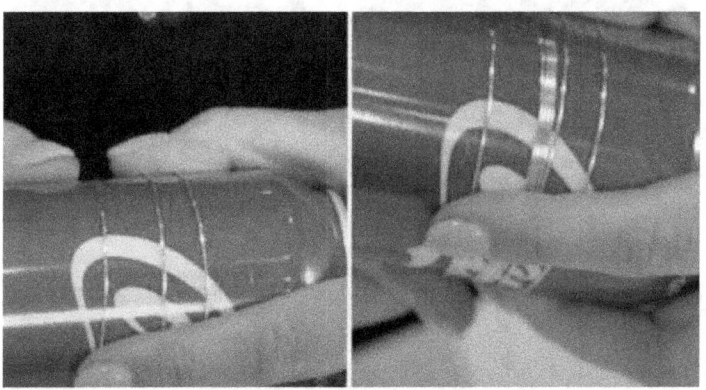

Step 2: Wrap the wire on the soda can, overhanging a few inches on the front side of the soda can. Then wrap the remaining wire to the right side of the soda can. Now, you can wrap the remaining wire side by side to create tight wraps. But ensure that the wraps are not

overlapping. There should be enough space between the wires, not so much. Just enough to prevent the wires from sitting on each other. Pass the can to your other hand and continue wrapping to ensure coordination and firmness. Once you have exhausted your wire, you can wiggle it out of the can and set it aside.

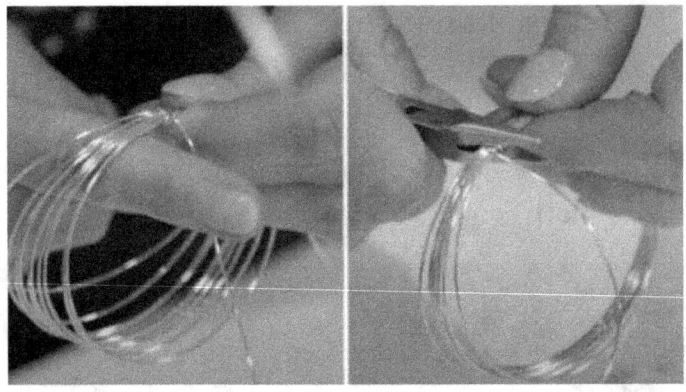

Step 3: Begin to bundle the wires together with your right hand and a little wire tail. Tie the wire over the bangle three or four times. Do not cut it off afterward; you will need it to add beads.

Then use the pliers; flat nose and round nose to adjust the shape of the bangle; you can squeeze a little hard. This is what will make the shape firm.

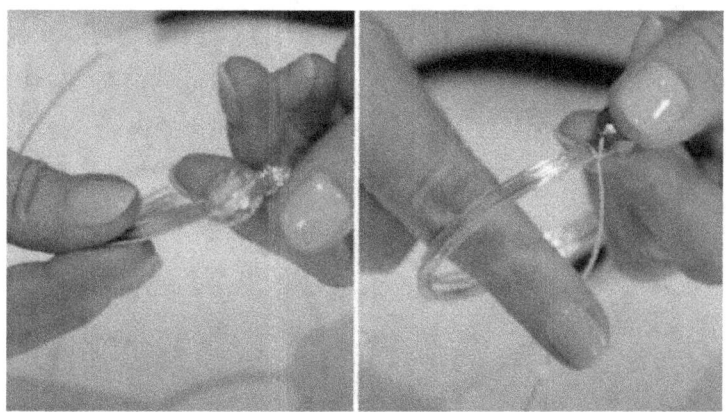

Step 4: Now you want to thread in your beads, it is best to use a bead with a flat base that would rest on the bangle. Thread in the bead and adjust it if you can manipulate it to rest over the edge of the bangle. After you have placed it firmly, you can start wrapping it to the right of the bead. The idea is that there should be good space in between the beads. So, after the first bead, you give space for the next bead to be added. Wrap three or four times around the bangle. You can flatten it with your flat nose plier. Now, you can cut off this wire.

Step 5: Add your second and third beads. Flip the bangle and start working with a wire that faces the opposite direction. Thread in your bead, wrap, adjust and secure. Then map the even spacing between the wires, wrap the bangles in a zig form so that you come to the third point in the bangle where you can wrap your third bead.

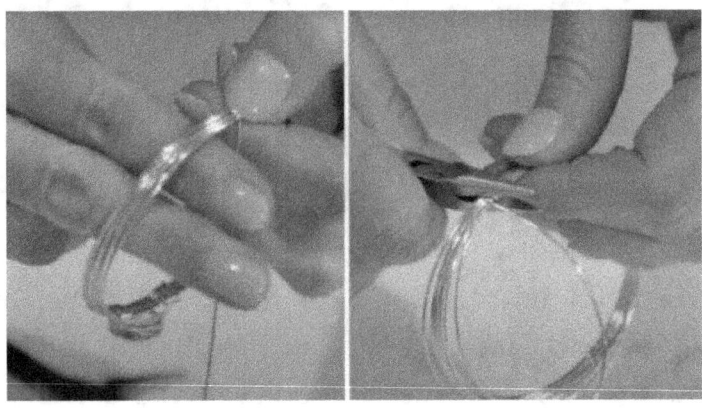

Step 6: Make four wraps just before the point you want to add the third bead, thread in the third bead and make tight wraps to secure it. Flatten your wrap with a flat nose plier.

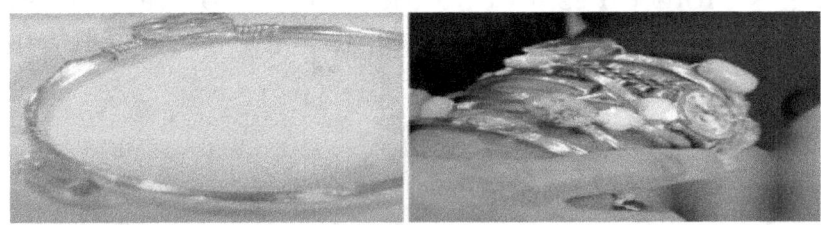

Step 7: Your bangle is ready; you can make as many bangles as you want to.

Swirled Wire Ear Cuff

Ear cuffs are a unique piece of jewelry that doesn't require your ear to be pierced. If you have a friend who loves jewelry but doesn't have her ears pierced, you can give this a good gift to such a person.

Tools and Supplies

- A wire of 19 gauge
- Pliers
- Beads

Instructions

Step 1: Cut the wire; measure out a piece of wire and cut it, ensure you cut the ends and make it straight.

Step 2: Bend the beginning of the wire to a small loop using your round nose pliers. Use the largest part of your plier to bend the small loop into a bigger one.

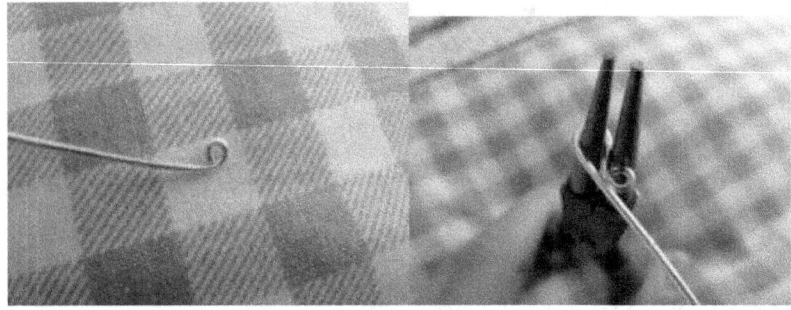

Step 3: Allow your wire to straighten a little, then make a big loop that is big enough to cover one side of your ear. After loop three, repeat the same process and make loop four.

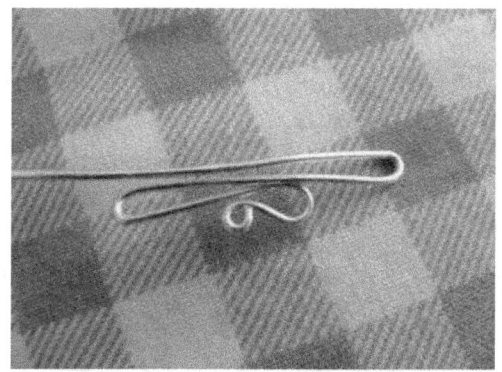

Step 4: Make a sixth wrap around the side of your pliers so that it sits basically with the small loop that you started with

Step 5: Keep making large wraps until your wire gets exhausted.

Step 6: Bend your wire in a certain position, and add your bead. Tighten it so you're sure it doesn't fall off

Step 7: Begin to make adjustments on the loops to make sure it fits. Make small and tight adjustments.

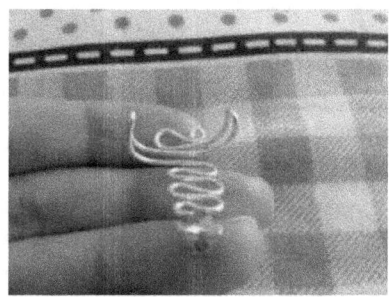

Wire Wrapped Headband

These headbands look just as amazing as pulling out a piece of jewelry from the jewelry box. It is unique and very beautiful.

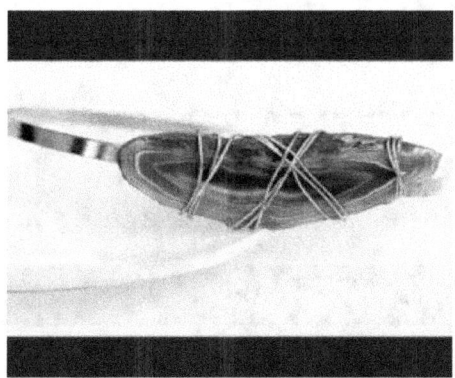

Tools and Supplies

- Wire; choose the level of thickness
- A metal headband

- Agate slab
- E6000 glue
- Wire cutters

Instructions

Step 1: Use glue to attach the agate slab to the headband at any position of your choice.

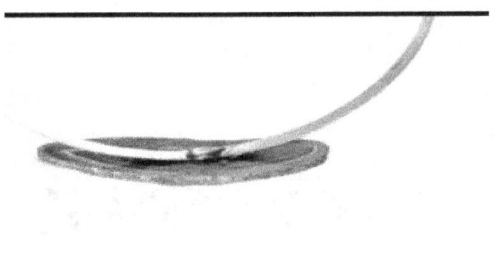

Step 2: Make a brief wrap around the headband. Start the wrap from the bottom of the agate slab.

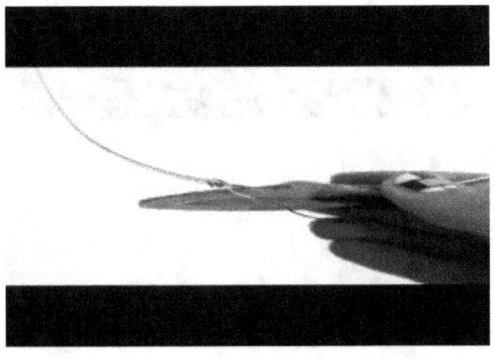

Step 3: Make a few more wraps around the slab and the headband

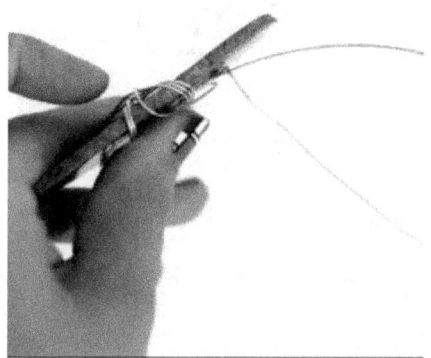

Step 4: Make more wraps until you are satisfied

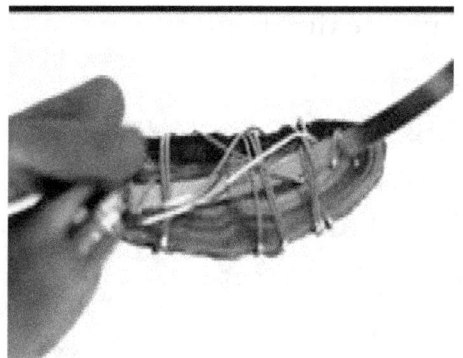

Step 5: To secure the wire, wrap it more times around the headband, then tuck it under the wire wrap, so there is no revealing sharp edge.

Your headband is ready.

Spiral Wire Bookmark

Tools and Supplies

- 16 or 18 gauge dead soft wire
- Charms
- Flush cutter
- Chain nose pliers
- Nylon jawed pillars
- Broad nose pliers
- Rubber mallet
- Steel block

Instructions

Step 1: Cut and measure out a length suitable for you, and cut the end of the wire with a flush cutter.

Step 2: Make a 90 degrees' bend with a broad nose plier. Just put the wire in the plier and hold it firmly while moving your hand along the wire slowly. After you make that bend, move the plier to make another 90 degrees.

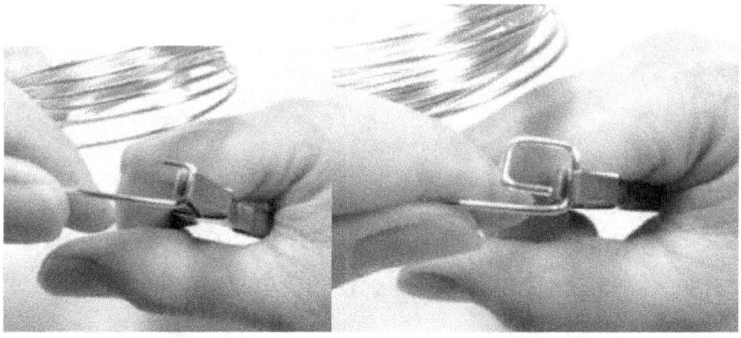

Step 3: You'll realize your first square is formed. Adjust the plier slightly so there is a little space before the next bend starts. Keep bending the wire as you go to create a square spiral. Thereafter curl the little end into a loop using the round nose pliers.

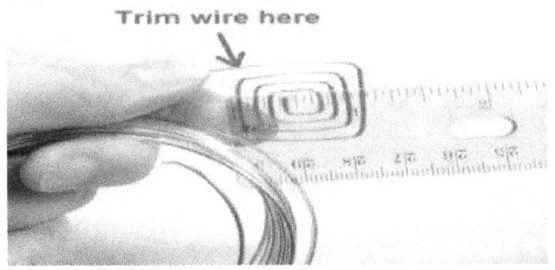

Step 4: Use the nylon hammer to work harden the spiral. You can place an object on the surface of the wire to prevent rough marks from the hammer.

Triangular spirals: This is almost made through the same process, but the angle used is smaller than the 90 angles.

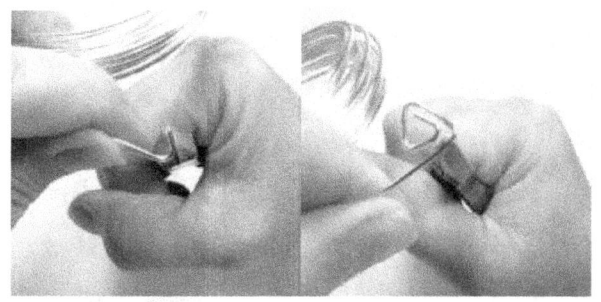

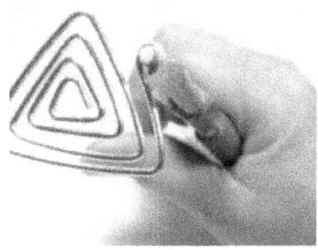

Round spirals: This spiral is made by moving the round nose plier along the wire to make circular or round shapes. Snip off the excess wire with a flush cutter. Your bookmark is almost as good as ready.

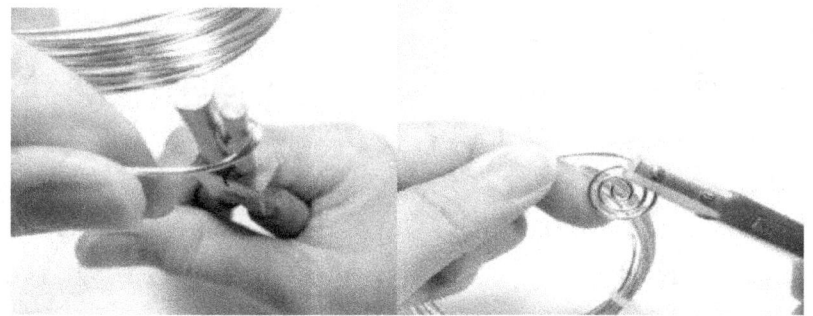

Use a nylon jawed design to make careful adjustments. You can open a loop and close it with a charm.

Wire Wrapped Bead Chain

Making bead chains could be enjoyable and exciting. You can create bead chains for necklaces, bracelets, earrings, and tassels. Bead chain is mostly made by linking beads on either side of the loops. If you are familiar with the basics of wire wrapping, you will find this project really easy. The method used here is referred to as the assembly line methodology.

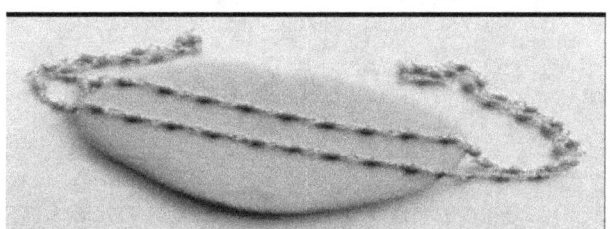

Tools and Supplies

- 2 inches of 24 g wire
- Flush cutter
- Beads
- Flat nose pliers
- Round nose pliers

Instructions

In this method, you repeat a step multiple times before moving on to the step in the process. An assembly line is really fast because you are going through the same process repeatedly and using the same tools consistently, so there is no need to switch tools or dive into a new process immediately. To make an assembly line, you'll need to prepare the second loops, cut the wires, join the connections and close up the loops.

Cut the wire for each bead link:

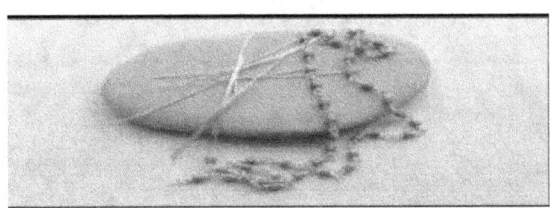

You need to decide how many beads will be in one link, then the length of wire needed to cover all the beads. So, you are also to decide the wire that will be used for each link. To make the link, measure and cut out your wire.

Wrap the wire on the link and trim out the excess wire. You can determine from there the length of wire needed to make the wraps. Add a few extra inches to allow for variation in bead size and enable you to flatten your wraps. Line the piece cut in the correct size and put the wire on the spool; you will then start a series of cutting and lining up. Cut and line up.

Make the loop for each bead link

Now, you have lined up the wires for each bead link; you have to make the loop for the links individually. When making a bead chain, join as many links as possible with one tool before putting it down. Hence, you will use only your round nose pliers to make loops for the links.

Wrap the loops from each bead link:

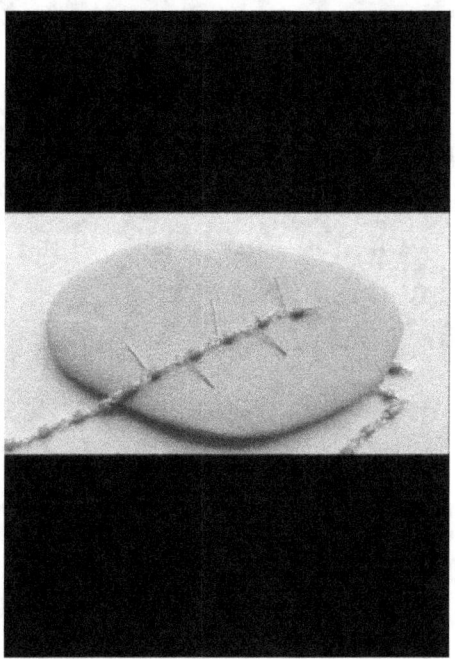

To complete the first loop, wrap the wrapping wire around the main wire, acting as a base wire or frame using pliers when wrapping, always tie the neck. Now you are ready to make your second major loop. Add in another bead. Add more beads to make more bead links.

Join the bead links, close the loops

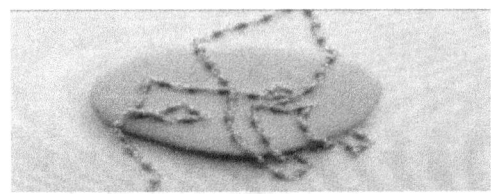

Start joining the links together with loops. After closing your loop, trim the excess wire or wire tails. Do not trim at any time in the linking or wrapping if you have a shortage of wire at the end. Also, adjust the wraps by tightening them and pressing them together with your arms. This is to avoid any extra wire that will encourage sliding beads.

Chapter 6

Wire Wrapped Jewelry Mistakes To Avoid

Wire wrapping jewelry could be exciting, but your whole project could come to nothing when mistakes are made. However, you can make some of these mistakes unconsciously and frustrate your learning process. The best solution is to address them ahead of time, so you can be wary of the possible cons and avoid them. When working with gemstone beads, you need to be extra careful

Here is a comprehensive list of mistakes to avoid;

- Starting too ambitious: this mistake is common with over-enthusiastic beginners. There could be temptations to take very complex projects while starting off to ascertain what degree of knowledge you have gathered. However, the danger here is that tough projects have their own technique and as a beginner, you probably haven't learned half of them. As much as you want to be creative, you can't just jump on any project you see just for the sake of it, or you would waste resources and get yourself demotivated. As a beginner, pick the projects you are sure you can handle. We have already listed fifteen unique projects for you. Start off with that. Then make consistent practice before you start trying other tougher projects.

- Improper wire cutting: practice how to use your wire cutters properly. There are two sides to your wire cutter; the front and the back. When you want to make flush cuts, use the back of your cutters. You are expected to make a pinch cut on very rare occasions. Also, learn and master the usage of every other tool like the pliers, crimpers and others

- Using expensive supplies in practicing pieces: when starting off as a beginner, you don't need to use high-quality materials in wrapping. You are expected to learn the basics. The basics here include making a loop, bails, curls, swirls and many other techniques. You can learn this with any wire. Using expensive supplies should be for only major projects, like when you want to make serious pieces. Don't use silver or gold wires when practicing.

- Poor uniformity in loops and final pieces: when you fail to uniform your loops, and your finishes, your work will definitely stand out as unprofessional. However, it is very possible to find yourself with loops of different sizes if you are not careful. One way to exercise such amount of care is by marking your jewelry with markers to record the point in the wire that will be used as a general measurement for all purposes. Other good alternatives are tapes and using necklace or bracelet board as a symmetrical template.

- Not using the right materials: in every good tutorial, you would come across the tools and supplies list, giving you hints on the type of tools and supplies you are expected to use. It is expedient that when starting as a beginner, you stick to these supplies list. Make sure you are following them accurately. Only when you have ascertained expertise and proficiency can you tweak the measurements and requirements to suit your expectations.

- Tool marks: when you exert too much pressure on your work, you might cause tool marks on the jewelry. Especially when making twirls and curls. You need to learn how to use tools carefully and less frequently if you will avoid tool marks totally. Of course, you will have times when you need these tools but only use them when needed; you can learn how to use your fingers as an alternative for most functions. In cases where you must use tools forcefully, you can consider putting a cloth in between the tool and the wire to reduce the effect of the tool scratches. You can also use tools with nylon tips when available. When you notice shallow scratches, you can use a needle file for scratching them out. Then give it a finer look by brushing it with a fine-grit jeweler's sandpaper. If it isn't too much work, you can file the body of your jewelry after wire wrapping.

- Broken wires: you can't imagine how much of a big problem it could be when your wire breaks while working on a project. Most times, a wire break would require that you undo a certain portion of your work and do it afresh on a new wire. Avoiding wire breaks could be tricky; however, you can reduce their chances of occurring by purchasing only quality wire with the appropriate gauge. The wire doesn't have to be too expensive, but it should have the necessary tensile strength and gauge size for the project you are working on. Consider annealing your wire before you begin; this will not remove the softness; it will make your wire pliable and less likely to break. When you break a wire, you can hide it by wrapping a light wire over it to join it back to the main wire. You can decide to wrap the whole of your base wires to make them appear more aesthetic.

- Base wire: if you are yet to master the art of shaping, you would need to rework the wire more times than necessary; hence you could mangle it. To cover up this mangling effect, coil the wire over all the exposed base wires. These could give your design a new tweak as well as hide the imperfections.

- Anneal the base wire: to make your base wires malleable, anneal them before you start working on them. This will make them softer and easier to work with. It will also reduce the turnout of tool marks.

- Go with the flow: sometimes, mistakes could open doors to explore your creativity and birth new designs. When you make mistakes in the shaping, assembling and adjusting of your wires, you just need to think of a new way your mistake can be converted to an idea. Sometimes, you really need to do not modify the mistake but adapt it and find a way to work it into real meaning. You could add another layer of wire, bend a wire, cut a wire, anneal, just do anything that brings life back to your jewelry. Most crafters share that some of their favorite designs were ideas born out of mistakes. You can make it happen also. Allow yourself to be creative.

The end... almost!

Hey! We've made it to the final chapter of this book, and I hope you've enjoyed it so far.

If you have not done so yet, I would be incredibly thankful if you could take just a minute to leave a quick review on Amazon

Reviews are not easy to come by, and as an independent author with a little marketing budget, I rely on you, my readers, to leave a short review on Amazon.

Even if it is just a sentence or two!

So if you really enjoyed this book, please...

\>> Click here to leave a brief review on Amazon.

I truly appreciate your effort to leave your review, as it truly makes a huge difference.

Chapter 7

Wire Wrapped Jewelry FAQs

1. What is the best wire gauge for wrapping stones?

The 20-gauge wire is commonly used for wrapping stones because of its malleability and firmness. It is not too stiff to be bent; neither is it too soft to break or lose its shape.

2. What jewelry projects can I do with wire wrapping?

There is almost no jewelry project that cannot be done with wire wrapping. You can wrap wire to create pieces of jewelry like pendants, necklaces, and crowns. Other common ones are ear cuffs, headpieces, bracelets, chokers, and tiaras. Other pieces of jewelry that can be made with wires include brooches. Feel free to use the techniques in this book to create any jewelry you want. You define your own limit when it comes to wire wrapping.

3. Why does my jewelry tarnish?

As amazing as your jewelry looks now, there is a sure tendency of it tarnishing. When a metal tarnishes, the top surface is washed away to reveal a poor underneath. This occurs when the jewelry is in contact with acids, oils, air, and moisture. Metals react adversely to these things and it has a way of depreciating the quality of the wire for worse and cause it to wear down. When a sterling silver wire comes in contact with moisture and sulfur in the atmosphere, it becomes dark tone. How quickly it wears and tarnishes is dependent on how well you use them, the air around you, the processes or materials used in making them, and the skin composition.

4. How to prevent a jewelry from tarnishing?

You might not be able to control several factors like the air composition around you and how it wears your material, but you can keep your certain practices to reduce the chances of your jewelry tarnishing.

Firstly, endeavor to keep your jewels dry. Remove them when washing your hands, applying lotion, spraying perfumes, or sweating. This is because the more liquid your metal comes in contact with, the more it tarnishes. When you notice they are wet by accident, pull them off and dry them thoroughly with a napkin.

Also, you need to learn to store it properly. When you are not wearing it, it should be in an air-tight closet or container. Most jewelry pieces come with velvet bags that you can use to protect your jewelry from sunshine and be safe from the harshness of the weather. A better saving or string option is a Ziploc bag. A 3M anti-tarnish strip is also a good vibe; it sucks all the air in the container you will be using, so the metal will not be able to oxidize.

Next, apply a jewelry protectant spray. This will help you fight the elements that cause tarnishing.

Finally, give the metal some break. Constant use could weary the wire. You can decide to let it be for as long as possible.

5. Can I store wire on a spool?

Most crafters store their wire in large spools. This is a good way to keep your wire for long in good condition without threats of tarnishing. Spools also help you to keep your wire tidy.

6. How to keep your figure 8 weave nice when making pendant bails?

Keeping your figure 8 neat and tidy could be a real-time struggle. However, below are few ways you can keep your figure 8. Firstly, ensure that you pick a gauge size that suits your pendant perfectly. Also your wire must be half hard. If what you have is a soft wire, harden it before you start working with it. Make accurate measurements before you start and endeavor to fold the wires properly. Use chasing hammers to hammer every fold into shape. As you weave, ensure to compress your rings firmly. Then shape your bail frame tightly. You should have a neat figure 8 weave with these tips.

7. How do I achieve a pretty hammered finish on my jewelry?

A jewelry hammer is not like every other hammer. You don't need force to create a great effect; what you need is precision. Planishing and peening are two techniques used in hammering jewelry. Planishing is a technique used in smoothening or flattening the wire peen that is used to create a more intense design or texture on the planished wire. You can't peen when you haven't planished. It is going to ruin the whole thing. Take your time to hit the wire slowly with the hammer in all the right places, don't be in a hurry to hammer and go.

8. How do you give your jewelry a shiny finish?

Most crafters use a rotary tumbler. There are different types and uses of this tumbler, but it is basically used in polishing the jewelry after wiring. It is a very small machine that you can carry everywhere and anywhere, especially when you want to travel. Although it could be messy when polishing, you are sure to get yourself a realm shiny finish when you are done. Again, this is no process where you hurry through to get results; you have to move the wire along the tumbler to polish the wire and shine it well.

9. How to keep your tumbler effective?

Don't use your tumbler on your jewelry when you haven't used it in a while. Clean your jewelry with dry clothes before cleaning it up with or polishing it with a tumbler. Also, periodically adjust the driver belt of your tumbler as you use it, or it will get worn out and stop turning.

10. What alternative can I use as a wire mandrel when making certain wire projects?

Jewelry mandrels are a must when you are making certain jewelry especially rings. When weaving small circular jewelry, you can use a knitting needle or copper pipe fittings as an alternative. For larger pieces of jewelry, you can get copper couplings. Other household items you can use in place of mandrels include; prescription bottles (for earrings and necklaces), wooden rolling pins, mixing bowls (torque-style necklace), flowerpots (larger necklaces), amongst others.

Conclusion

It is necessary to make an extensive budget before starting off wire-wrapped jewelry making, especially if you are working on something huge. Wire wrapping Jewelry is fun when you have all the right tools and supplies to make a project. You will be doing yourself a lot of harm if you try to use the wrong tools or supplies when carrying out a project. Most crafters try to get cheap tools to begin, but the testimonies are sure; you are bound to get frustrated by your result. No one is saying you should get the most expensive tool in the market, but in this book, we have listed all the necessary tools you should get and their descriptions. Whatever it would cost, make that investment now and you'll be happy you did.

Also, ensure to master all the techniques discussed; don't start any project on assumptions, and you will certainly be ready for a fulfilling wire wrapping journey. With the knowledge encapsulated herein and the step-by-step project instructions to get you started, you can be assured that you are well-prepped to make your first wire-wrapped jewelry successfully. However, don't be afraid of failing; only be careful to review your mistakes with the explained steps discussed in this book to know what you missed. And when you do, get yourself back on that project and continue grinding. I'm rooting for you.

www.ingramcontent.com/pod-product-compliance
Lightning Source LLC
Chambersburg PA
CBHW071417070526
44578CB00003B/588